AWAKENING INTO
ONENESS

AWAKENING INTO
ONENESS

The Power of Blessing
in the Evolution
of Consciousness

ARJUNA ARDAGH

SOUNDS TRUE
Boulder, Colorado

Sounds True, Inc.
Boulder, CO 80306

© 2007 Arjuna Ardagh

SOUNDS TRUE is a trademark of Sounds True, Inc.

All rights reserved. Published 2007.
Printed in Canada

Jacket design by Lisa Kerans
Interior design by Karen Polaski
Illustration on page 50 by Patty Arnold

Photos on pages vi and viii are used by permission from the guides of the
Oneness University.

ISBN 978-1-59179-573-5

Library of Congress Cataloging-in-Publication Data

Ardagh, Arjuna.

   Awakening into oneness : the power of blessing in the evolution of

consciousness / Arjuna Ardagh.

      p. cm.

   ISBN 978-1-59179-573-5 (hardcover)

   1. Diksa. 2. Religious awakening--Hinduism. I. Title.

BL1226.82.D55A73 2007

294.5'38--dc22

                          2006101647

CONTENTS

The Oneness University

The Oneness Temple

BLESSING FROM ONENESS UNIVERSITY

Awakening into Oneness is not the story of one person or a group of people. It is the story of a phenomenon that is sweeping across the globe, awakening millions in its path. Its relevance is for all time and for all people, irrespective of their religious convictions. This book has the potential to awaken the reader to the awesome and intelligent power of the Oneness Blessing, as reading the book itself delivers an experience of Blessing. It has the power to awaken the seeker to the eternal and immanent presence of the Divine and to initiate a process of awakening that eventually culminates in the realization of the Oneness of all life.

We at Oneness University know *Awakening into Oneness* will be instrumental in the emergence of a new human being with a global outlook, free of all divisions—racial, national, religious, or otherwise.

Acharya Anandagiri
Oneness University
January 2007

Sri Bhagavan
Founder of the Oneness University

Sri Amma
Founder of the Oneness University

FOREWORD

I accepted to write a few words to introduce Arjuna Ardagh's book because its topic is of extraordinary importance for each of us individually, as well as for all of us collectively. Moreover, it meshes perfectly with my theoretical conceptions and with my own experience. I went to Oneness University in 2006 and had three weeks of meditation, as well as personal encounters with Bhagavan. But this is not an autobiographical essay; the reader will find abundant personal accounts in the chapters that follow. I merely wish to note that what is recounted in this book corresponds to what I experienced myself, and it also corresponds to the results of the research I have conducted over the past two decades.

These considerations give me good reasons to take seriously the experiences described in this book. However, these experiences should be taken seriously by everyone. The correspondence of the lived experience of now quite a sizable number of people in nearly all parts of the world with the insights we are gaining at the cutting edge of the sciences is of great theoretical as well as practical interest. When we add to this that the spread of this kind of experience is likely to be a factor in choosing the shape of our future, we get excellent reasons, indeed, for reading and pondering the ideas and experiences described in the chapters that follow.

Let me summarize why I believe that this book merits the reader's full attention.

1. **Reality.** The experiences it recounts are far from ordinary, yet they are not illusory; they are rooted in the physical reality of the cosmos;

2. **Urgency.** The spread of these experiences in society is in the interest of the entire human family—in its most concrete and immediate interest.

These are big claims, and they deserve further elucidation.

The "Oneness experience"—popularly but somewhat misleadingly said to have "enlightenment" as its goal—is grounded in physical processes that are just as real as the perception of light, color, and sound, but they are conveyed by the reception of a different kind of information by the brain. The experiences are made possible by a balanced state of the brain (though they are not caused by this state in a mechanistic sense). One aspect of this state has been researched in connection with receiving the Oneness Blessing and exposure to the dasas who give Blessings and have presumably achieved the balanced state.

The detailed cerebral mechanisms that constitute a balanced brain state call for further neurophysiological investigation, but one feature is already clear.

The widespread experience of deep prayer and meditation—and of altered states of consciousness in general—provides evidence that in altered states of consciousness, the classical information processing of the left cerebral hemisphere is no longer dominant. The brain does not operate predominantly in the classical mode, whereby one item of consciousness follows others in a linear sequence, and perception is not limited to signals conducted by the bodily senses. In altered states of consciousness, the gestalt-perceiving, "parallel-processing" operating modality of the right hemisphere comes to the fore. This entails opening the receptivity of the brain to a range of information well beyond the sensory signals received through eye, ear, nose, palate, and skin.

In the cerebral states that underlie altered states of consciousness, the brain operates in a non-classical mode: as a "macroscopic quantum system." It shifts from being an EM-wave and photon-wave receiver, to operating as a quantum-field transceiver. It receives, as well as sends, information in the form of holographic patterns in the quantum wave-field that, as an element in the quantum vacuum, underlies all things in the universe. (I have called this universal information field the Akashic Field, for its effect recalls the ancient concept of Akasha, the cosmic medium that interconnects and records all things in space and time.)

In commonsense terms, altered states of consciousness liberate us from the ego-limited condition whereby we view the world through five slits in the tower—they open for us the roof to the sky.

Opening the roof is facilitated, even if it is not uniquely caused, by the experience of receiving the Oneness Blessing. In turn, the sensitivity of individuals to this Blessing is facilitated by undergoing the consciousness-evolution regime Bhagavan calls "Oneness process." The Oneness process enhances the effect of the Oneness Blessing, and thus helps individuals to achieve the altered states of consciousness in which their brain operates as a macroscopic quantum system.

Is the opening of the brain, and hence of the consciousness associated with it, to quantum fields of major consequence? I believe it is, since these fields link the brain and consciousness of individuals with the world around them. They permit the discovery, or more exactly the re-discovery, of these linkages, for they were known to traditional peoples and are still known to non-Western cultures and to spiritual people wherever they live. The experience of connection with others and with nature has been described by religious leaders, mystics, and spiritually versed or inclined people, whether they had entered altered states through prayer or through meditation. They are the essence of the "awakening into Oneness," the consciousness evolution alluded to in the title of this book.

Rediscovering our links with the world around us is important for us as individuals: it makes us more whole, more sensitive, and at the same time more balanced persons. It is extraordinarily important for us collectively. This is because at the root of the problems now faced by humanity is the outmoded, egoically constrained consciousness. It prompts narrowly self-centered values, beliefs, and behaviors. Bhagavan is correct when he states that there is only one cause for human problems, and that is the sense of separateness—the sense that the world can be divided into "me" and "not me." Of course, this separation is not limited to the dichotomy of "me" and "the rest of the world," but is moderated by various forms of identification that are not purely egoic: with family, community, nation, culture, and even enterprise. But the current forms of identification clearly fall short of the global identification we need to survive as a species. This identification can only be based on the lived experience of oneness—of our connection with each other, and with nature.

In recent books, I have discussed why I believe that nothing short of a global level of identification with all members of the human family, and with the biosphere that is the human family's life-support system, can give a reasonable chance of weathering the coming decades without major catastrophe. I shall not repeat the argument here—the evidence, in any case, is clear and available to everyone. It is enough to state the conclusion I reached after years of studying the steadily growing problems and challenges facing the human community. I can sum it up in a single sentence: unless there are fundamental changes in the way we conduct our affairs on this planet, the chances that all six-and-a-half billion of us would survive the next decade are extremely slim.

Every BAU ("business-as-usual") scenario leads to a population collapse, due to one of several root causes: climate change producing drought that makes it impossible for up to a third of the human population to grow adequate food to cover its basic needs; the lowering of water tables and the concurrent pollution of the water resources of over half the world's population; the rise of the sea level threatening the coastal populations that make up over a fourth of the population; the famine that results from extreme poverty as well as from the degradation of the environment, and has as a consequence the spread of debilitating diseases—and the woefully inadequate development of the body and brain of the children who make up the bulk of the next generation; and the maverick or organized violence—the terrorism and the warfare—that results from increasing stress, poverty, lack of information and education, religious and ethnic intolerance, and short-sighted response to conflicts of economic interests.

BAU scenarios are deadly. Can they be avoided? The answer is, they can: we have the money (even a part of what we spend on the military would cover the requirements); we have the energy (we are using but a tiny fraction of the solar radiation that reaches the surface of the planet); and we have the technology (a variety of alternative energy technologies and technologies of sustainable resource use are already on line).

What is keeping us, then, from shifting from a BAU to a sustainable scenario? Only a failure of will. Why do we lack the economic, the political, and the civic will? Because, for the most part, we fail to perceive the critical nature of our situation. Why do we fail to perceive it? Evidently because we are still under the spell of an obsolete consciousness, with narrow perceptions, short time-horizons, and the assumption that everyone is separate from everyone else and is interested only in pursuing his or her immediate material goals and interests.

How can we change this dangerous condition? The answer is clear: by changing ourselves as a way to change the world. But how can we change ourselves? Here is where the critical importance of the Oneness Blessing and the Oneness process comes in. The most reliable, lasting, and effective way to change ourselves is to evolve our consciousness.

One last question: How much time do we have to reach a more evolved consciousness? The answer may be shocking to many people: for the human family as a whole, the time is less than a decade. The date I have arrived at is the same that Bhagavan had envisaged: the end of 2012. This is not mere coincidence. A major shift in the tenor of human life on this planet by the end of the year 2012 has been predicted by a surprising number of cultures, from the Mayan and the Cherokee to the Indian. This date appears to be deeply etched in the collective unconscious of contemporary humanity, and both Bhagavan and I have sensed it. In my case, I came to it as an intuitive insight before I did the empirical research and the calculations. The latter merely confirmed the insight, with a margin of error that is not likely to exceed a few years in one direction or the other.

Change yourself to change the world, and thus make 2012 not the opening phase of a collective catastrophe but the prelude to a new, peaceful, and sustainable civilization: this, in a nutshell, is my message, and the message of this book that shows us how all of us can "awaken into Oneness."

Ervin Laszlo, Ph.D.
19 December 2006

CHAPTER ONE

THE DIAMOND
EARRINGS

When my old friend Micki Karlholm sent me an e-mail to announce that he had just returned from India, where he had found the key to permanent enlightenment, I was at a loss. How could I possibly explain to him just how completely not interested I was?

Micki is the original founder of the No-Mind Festival in Sweden, and I have known him for many years. He is one of the kindest and most deeply honest people I know. So I was both surprised and disappointed to see him swallowed up by another Indian cult. I thought we were both over that one.

A few days later, we spoke on the phone. He told me this simple story.

For twelve years, Micki had been married to a woman from Denmark. They had children together. Throughout the marriage, he was always promising to buy her a pair of diamond earrings. "Just wait a little while longer. I will make us so much money that you will get your earrings. You wait and see." She waited and waited, and finally, they got divorced. No earrings.

Micki told me that while he was visiting this place in India, they did some kind of processes on him that affected his brain. I imagined scalpels and tubes and wires and machines and dubious hygiene. In one of these processes, for example, they helped him to feel all the pain he had unconsciously caused to other people. Micki was able to feel that simple broken heart—all the disappointment—he had left with his ex-wife in Denmark. When he returned from India to his native Sweden, he went straight to a jeweler and bought her the earrings. He drove without stopping to Denmark and knocked on her door. He offered her first an apology, and then the earrings.

"Micki," I said to him, "now I am interested." This was not a story of peak enlightenment experiences displaced from ordinary life; this was not another obsession with higher states. This was a story about my friend Micki becoming a more decent human being. It was right in line with everything I was passionate about.

At that time, I was just coming to the end of three years of research for my book *The Translucent Revolution,* a thoroughly overambitious survey of twenty-first-century spirituality. I conducted hundreds of interviews and finally managed to distill millions of words down to a mere 520-page pamphlet. The book came out in the early summer of 2005 to the usual circus of press interviews, talks in bookstores, and TV and radio shows. "It's six a.m. here, folks, in rural Wisconsin, and our guest today is . . . Arhooh Aghaaaaar. (Did I say that right? Hell, never mind.) So, Mr. Ahaaaar, what is this trans . . . luminous thing? Does it have anything to do with that thing Tom Cruise does in L.A.? I mean, what did you make of his outburst on Oprah? . . . Let's talk about *that.*"

I needed a break. And just as often happens when something is coming your way whether you like it or not, I kept on bumping into that same brain-changing thing Micki had told me about. At that time it was called *deeksha.* Today it is more commonly called the Oneness Blessing. No surgery or beeping machines were involved. A Oneness Blessing giver would put his or her hands on your head for a few minutes, initiating a powerful rebalancing of energy in the brain. One of the first Westerners to be trained to do this gave someone a ride to our house and then ended up staying over. And so it was that my wife and I got our first-ever Oneness Blessing. If we had experienced flashing lights or firework displays or visions of ascended masters, we might have been less attracted. What we did find was a delicious immersion in the same silence, peace, spaciousness, and causeless love that we both knew to be the essence of spiritual longing and practice. Here was a dropping back into that presence in just a minute, with just a touch on the head. The simple fragrance of home. After that, wherever we went, there seemed to be a blessing giver there, too. Were these guys following us?

The final straw came when I heard directly from the Oneness University in India, where all these people had been trained. It seems the university's founder had read *The Translucent Revolution* and liked it. Would I like to come for a visit?

My wife and I both certainly needed a holiday. Was it expensive? Come as our guests. Would we get our own room, no dormitory? No problem. Could we rest as much as we liked? Twenty-four hours a day. Is it a quiet place? Middle of nowhere. Can we do our own thing, be undisturbed? You can be totally silent.

They were good to their word. The campus was situated in a mango grove near low-lying mountains. For most of the time, all we could hear were the chirping of birds and the croaking of frogs. We slept and we slept; we ate some really quite tasty Indian food, took a short walk, and then we slept again. The whole place was run by young Indian men and women called *dasas*. They all wore white and were extraordinarily energetic and in permanently unflappable good moods, despite the fact that they seemed to never sleep. Our dasa (literally, "guide"), Pragyanand, would show up soon after eight in the morning to see if we would like a deeksha, as it is called in India. Sure, why not? It's not like we had a packed schedule or anything. Each day the deeksha would have a specific intention, such as balancing the body, clearing old relationships, or, as was the case for Micki, helping one to feel pain one had caused to others. One day early on, for example, our young dasa announced that we would receive a deeksha to clear impressions left over from the relationship with the mother. I was skeptical. Back in the 1970s, I had beaten cushions and screamed primal screams. Later, I did est, hypnotherapy, psychotherapy, even colon therapy. I thought I had cleaned out pretty good, and I really had not thought about childhood for more than a decade.

Pragyanand did his deeksha; it took only a minute or two. Then he stood up to leave with the words "Now you rest." Rest? Are you crazy? We had just been sleeping for fourteen hours straight, plus we took three naps yesterday. "I tell you the . . . very . . . . last . . . . . thing . . . . . . I . . . . need . . . . is . . . . to . . . ."

We were gone, as though the bed suddenly had powerful magnets installed in it. And then a powerful stream of images started to emerge, things I had not thought of for decades. The way my mother brushed her hair before we were leaving to go out . . . the smell of the laundry detergent . . . the time she locked herself in her room, and the neighbor had to come and . . . It went on and on, for several hours. As the images continued, I could actually feel things happening in my brain, as though it were being massaged from inside. And then it stopped, just as it had started, for both my wife and me at the same time. We got up and walked around. Things were quite normal, except that later in the day, someone would casually say the word "mother," and it provoked a deep resonance of love and gratitude. It was as though there had been furniture there before, and now it was gone, and gratitude had filled its place. "I love my mother"—that was all that remained. The rest was a story that served no purpose.

It went on and on like that. A short deeksha, a powerful inward release something like a shamanic journey, and then more and more space, simplicity, love—the return to the natural state where things are just as they are, and there is no commentary saying it should be any different than it is.

Toward the end of our stay at the Oneness University, I sat down with our guide. "This is really quite powerful stuff, you know?" I told him. He smiled that unflappable smile again. "I know," he grinned. Just twenty-five years old, he had the innocence of a child and the deep wisdom of a sage. During this three-week vacation, I had watched him be fully present with world-famous musicians, politicians, writers, and seminar leaders from all over the world. I had watched him greet their moments of ecstasy and agony with equal calm. He was around from six in the morning till way after midnight. I was seriously impressed. "I don't think people in the rest of the world fully appreciate the power of what is happening here. You guys really need someone to write a good book," I told him. "Maybe," he said, and smiled.

A couple of days later, he got back to me. "Thank you for your idea. We would love for *you* to write the book."

• • •

There were several things that really impressed me on that first visit to the Oneness University. The first were those 170 dasas. I have spent a good deal of my life around organized spirituality. The situation has always been more or less the same. A great teacher, great teachings, wonderful practices, meditations or prayers, and then among the followers, there was always a certain degree of politics. Who could get higher in the organization? Who had the power? During my three-week stay at the university, I looked under every rock and behind every bush. Where was the politics? I could not find it, even after an exhaustive search. What I found instead was an extraordinary quality of oneness: people living together, working together, being together as many bodies but one heart, one consciousness. I saw it not only among the dasas, but also with the security personnel, the women caring for the garden, the drivers.

The second thing that impressed me about the Oneness University were the Oneness Blessings themselves. I have practiced many kinds of meditation over the years, as well as prayers, physical exercises, and other practices. It was always somewhat hit-and-miss. You could do the same practice day after day, and sometimes you would hit the jackpot and be drenched in peace, while many times you were left wading through the mud of the mind. The Oneness Blessing was different. It was fast, clean, and accurate. It seemed to hit the mark every time and deliver the goods. Moreover, it seemed to have an intelligence of its own; it knew where to go and what was needed, whether it was healing, releasing memories, or just deepening silence.

The third thing that moved me was the vision out of which all of this was arising. They had a plan. Not only a plan for a few meditation veterans like me and my friends, but also a plan for transforming global consciousness. It was a plan that may sound ridiculously optimistic at first hearing, but it had caught the attention and support of visitors from the Vatican as well as of Muslim leaders, presidents of countries, musicians, writers, and Hollywood celebrities. It is a plan you will hear more about in these pages, a plan that might slowly grow on you.

I left my first visit to the Oneness University armed with both enthusiasm and skepticism. Was this just another workshop high? What happens to the Oneness people once they get back to their jobs and houses and kids and busy lives? This book is the answer to those questions. I have interviewed more than three hundred Blessing givers and receivers from all over the world. Some of the people you will meet in these pages are celebrities or household names. Many are ordinary people leading ordinary lives. I have talked with doctors who give the Oneness Blessing to their patients, with CEOs who have brought the Blessing to their companies, and with teachers who have brought it to their classes. I have talked with people who see the Oneness Blessing as the saving grace that has transformed their lives, as well as to others who are highly skeptical and critical. I returned to the Oneness University in the summer of 2006 to research this book and to make a movie, and I received an extraordinary level of cooperation and openness. I was able to conduct more than six hours of interviews with the university's founder, Sri Bhagavan, as well as with his wife, Sri Amma, who had never previously given an interview. I was given free access to all the operations of the university and was allowed to wander freely through all its varied activities.

Writing this book has been like trying to paint a picture of a ballet. Every time you look up from the canvas, things have moved. This phenomenon is known simply as "deeksha" in India, the land rich in mystical heritage where it started. During the time that I was conducting the interviews for this book, it was known by the same word throughout the world also. As it has spread rapidly throughout other countries, it became clear that it needed a new name, no longer tied to any particular tradition. It has now come to be known as "Oneness Blessing," or "Oneness Deeksha." Throughout the text I will use these words interchangeably, although they all refer to the same simple magical touch of the divine, the same the world over. In quoting from the hundreds of interviews I conducted in India, with Amma, Bhagavan, and the staff of the Oneness University, I have retained the word "deeksha." In quoting people from Western countries, where the new term is now used, and for the narrative of the book, written in my own voice, I have used the new term "Oneness Blessing."

This book is neither an evangelical text of conversion nor an exposé. It is an attempt to summarize the effects of a movement that has spread extraordinarily quickly all over the world and affected millions of people. You will hear from many people in this book who feel their lives have been completely transformed. You will also hear of the five major criticisms aimed at the Oneness movement, which are lobbed daily across the Internet like custard pies. You will have to come to your own conclusions based upon what you read here. You might run to your nearest Oneness Blessing giver or even wind up jumping on a plane for the next Oneness training in India, or you might dismiss what you read here as just another cult. Whatever your conclusions, this has proven to be the fastest-growing spiritual phenomenon in living memory. Although many continue to be attracted to the Oneness Blessing while many others back away in disbelief, this is something that few will be able to ignore in the years ahead.

CHAPTER TWO

THE GOLDEN BALL

Father, there's a golden man in my heart, and he talks to me."

The school director looked up from the papers on his desk at Krishna, his eleven-year-old son, and smiled. The director had a round and gentle face, big cheeks, and eyes that smiled all the time, even when the rest of his face was at rest.

"What does he say to you, Krishna?" asked the director. His voice was warm and deep, conveying a feeling of security, that all was well and at peace with the world.

"He tells me different things, Father." Krishna paused. He knew he could not talk like this to anyone else—they would laugh or call him crazy. But with his father, it was different. It had been like that for as long as he could remember. "I ask him to give me different experiences, and he gives them to me. This morning I was hungry, and I asked him for an apple. Right away, I could taste the apple, and then my hunger was satisfied. Sometimes he tells me what will happen, and then it comes true." The director paused and looked intensely at his son. "I'm not making this up, Father. It's completely real, and it's there all the time."

"I know, Krishna," said the director, slowly. "I know. From how you describe it, this sounds like you are having a vision of Prajapathi. It happens sometimes that people have visions like this. It's a very special thing, Krishna, a very great blessing. You must cherish it and tell me often what is happening."

Krishna loved his father more than just as a father. He was his best friend, too. Krishna never questioned what his father said, as he trusted his father more than he trusted anyone. He had never heard of Prajapathi, but if his father said it was a good thing, he knew it was so. All the children at the school loved the man they knew as "Director Sir" and his wife, Padmavati. The students raced in their direction amid peals of laughter whenever there was a chance to be with them. No one ever felt judged; everyone could be him- or herself.

Krishna raised his hands, placed them together on his heart in the traditional greeting of namaste to his father, and ran back outside.

He ran past the big sign that greeted visitors to the school: *A Foundation for World Awakening*. He ran past the bottlebrush tree, with its bright red flowers. He ran past the large Buddha statue in the middle of the lawn and past more signs that had been erected around the school: *"Your thoughts are not your thoughts. Your mind is not your mind,"* read one, and *"Man is mad. Enlightenment is the natural state,"* read another. Krishna kept running, past the whitewashed buildings with their red-tiled roofs, past the mango trees. There was only one thing now on his mind: cricket.

"Krishna, where have you been?" cried a shrill voice. It belonged to Giri, Krishna's best friend, one year his senior. A small and thin boy, Giri had eyes that permanently sparkled with enthusiasm. Giri's mother had died when he was seven, leaving only his father to care for him. He would often remain at the school, even during vacation time, with Krishna and his parents. The two boys became inseparable, like brothers. "We're just starting a match. Come on, Krishna, you'll miss the calling out of the teams." The two friends ran together now, past another sign inscribed with the words of the great Lebanese poet Kahlil Gibran— *"Your children are not your children"*—and onto the open space that served as a cricket field, where at least fifty other boys had gathered.

• • •

Jeevashram was no ordinary school. The director had founded it in 1984 to provide an alternative form of education. He and his wife saw that the current educational system was destroying the child. They wanted to create a school where children could truly flower, discover who they really were. The primary focus, right from the beginning, was on spiritual maturity: to free the child of the sense of a separate self and of self-centered preoccupations. They aimed to create an atmosphere free of fear, free of competition.

They started out with nothing, just a vision. They found some land in rural Andhra Pradesh, far from civilization, which they took on a lease. The first year, they had a handful of students and just one building. They had initially planned for one classroom with tables and a separate dormitory with bunk beds. Lack of funds, however, meant the two had to be combined into one building, and the director invented the "tablot," a table by day that transformed, with the rolling out of a thin cotton mattress, into a cot by night. The children loved it.

After just a few years, the school had grown to house 180 residential students, both boys and girls. It also welcomed two hundred poor local children from surrounding villages, most of whom came in every day without fees. The director oversaw everything: gardens were planted, he erected the signs around the campus, and that one original building grew into a sprawling campus of dormitories, classrooms, and dining and meeting rooms. Children excelled at gardening, woodwork, music, and crafts, as well as the more traditional disciplines.

The director took charge of the school's spiritual direction, and invited a friend he had known since childhood to become the principal who could care more for the academic side. The director gave classes on meditation, on different spiritual disciplines, and on philosophy. He encouraged the children to think for themselves, to ponder deeper philosophical questions for days at a time. Sometimes he conducted classes in mathematics—in which he himself had graduated—or in history. He also hired a headmaster, who coordinated with government authorities and hired other specialty teachers.

The school conformed to all the government standards, but the children were never placed under academic pressure of any kind. They were not ranked or graded, and no child was ever kept back in a grade for lack of academic performance. All the emphasis was placed on the quality of relationships among the children, their relationships with their parents, and their state of internal happiness and well-being. The teachers were instructed never to scold the children or to punish them. The headmaster would go to great lengths to find teachers who could love the children as well as teach them and who were themselves experiencing internal freedom and joy. The experiment was a huge success: by the time the children graduated, their academic grades were far superior to those of students in other schools. Many of those children today have become doctors, engineers, and business leaders.

When Giri was admitted to the school, he was only nine years old. Each year, only seventeen new residential students were admitted. When Giri's father took his son to meet the director for the first time, he had different ambitions for his son. "I would like my boy to make it to IIT (Indian Institute of Technology). That is the best school for engineering and technology in the country. I want him to become a successful software engineer. Can you manage that?" he demanded of the school director. The director looked at him with those same calm, laughing eyes.

"I am sure we could do that, yes. I am sure it could happen. But first I have one question for you: What if your son has a different passion? What happens if he prefers to work with herding cattle, or he wants to work with clay and be a potter? What happens if that is what will make him happy? Are you also prepared for that? Will you still love him then? Will you still support his vision?"

Giri's father was quiet for a few moments. He had not expected this question from the director. He had assumed they would just want the tuition payment, and that would be that. Finally, he agreed that he could accept these terms. "Applicant admitted," grinned the director, as he stamped the application form with a flourish.

All the children remember Jeevashram as a magical place. Physically, it was quite simple, made up of simple concrete buildings. The director and his wife lived in a simple whitewashed building with very little furniture. They had no vehicle. Jyoti, a young girl who had joined the school the same year as Giri, remembers:

From the very beginning, it felt so good to be there. Physically, it was such a beautiful place. I did not consciously know what silence was then. At least, I didn't know to define it as silence. Right away, there was a feeling of great space and a sense of awe. The feeling of great space was outside—it was a big campus—but it was inside also, inside me. It was filling me up with peace. We felt so much love and affection from the director and his wife. Within three or four days, I was resolving, "I will be with them forever." The director's wife looked after the general administration, and she also took care of the girls. She was like our mother, our best friend. She was somebody who would totally build us up, who made everything possible for us. There was no limitation in her presence.

From the very beginning, it became a normal thing for children to have mystical experiences. Prayer became very strong for them; they got used to the fact that whatever they asked for came to them. Then, in the summer of 1989, things dramatically deepened. Mathew* was a very serious and academic boy from a Christian home. His prayers were always to do better on his exams. One day, the director called him in to the office. "Your prayers are so strong to do well in class," said the director. "Why don't you pray that grace descends into you, and you become enlightened?" Mathew did as the director suggested. Later in the day, when he walked into the dining hall, he was like a sage. His eyes were deep and penetrating; his body movements slow and deliberate, like a dancer's. He could hardly speak. The next day, he explained to the director that a huge golden ball had appeared before him and descended into him. The ball had spoken a word to him, in a language he did not understand.

A few days later, exactly the same thing happened to Chandra, one of the more mischievous students. He loved to play with frogs and often played jokes on people. It gets very hot in southern India in the spring, and during a math class one afternoon, the children were getting sleepy. Chandra also suddenly felt a golden ball descend through the top of his head and settle into his heart. He was immediately drenched in silence, in a feeling of ecstatic peace that filled him completely. When the class ended and the children filed out into the hot afternoon, Chandra remained in his place, still absorbed in his rapture. It took several hours until he could move again, and when he did, he was transformed completely. Soon after, almost the same thing happened to two other children.

---

*Name has been changed to protect the privacy of the individual.

One afternoon in August, the school director called Krishna back into the simple room where he sometimes met with people. The room was empty except for a long, low table in the middle. The torrential monsoon rains were falling outside. "Now we will see if it is possible for you to transfer your experience of the golden being to others," he told his son. Krishna admitted he had no idea how to do that, but the school director reassured him that he would not need to do anything; it would all happen on its own. After some time had passed, he called Jyoti in to join them. She was about thirteen at the time. Years later, she recalls what occurred:

The director just said, "Krishna will give you something; take it." There was no other explanation given. Then he told me to close my eyes. Krishna laid his hands on my head for just a few moments, and then he took them back and sat. All that I could see was a huge light entering into me. As he laid his hands, there was an awakening, a fire. It shot from down under, intense heat spread up to the crown of my head, and then slowly each of the chakras in my body started blossoming. I saw all kinds of different deities located inside my body. The entire thing seemed to me as though it lasted a really long time. By the clock, it happened within two to three minutes. When I opened my eyes, I was dazed. I didn't understand what had happened to me. I went back to the dormitory, and still when I closed my eyes, there were visions of deities. It seemed to continue. What he had given me was still there, inside my body, like a seed. It was slowly unfolding itself.

A few weeks later, I went home for the vacation in September. I was reading a book, and I lay down and closed my eyes. An immense sweetness came over my heart, in the middle of my chest. I could not believe it. I saw the director in my heart. There was Sir; he was inside me. After a few days, I saw him with his wife there, too. The energy kept exploding. I felt it continuing from that day till now. Love had taken possession. Suddenly, I had become a poet; everything had changed. It was divine love that was consuming me. After the vacation, I knocked on the director's door. "Please, Sir, I'm able to see you inside my heart. You talked to me." All that he said was, *"It happens, sometimes." That was all.*

That fall, Krishna gave this same "deeksha" to many of the children. They would queue up and say, "Please touch me, please touch me." And right away, extraordinary experiences would start to unfold. It became a fairyland, a magical place. They were from all kinds of religious and ethnic backgrounds. The Christian children would see Jesus after the deeksha, and feel his love, and come to know him in a personal way. The Muslims would meet the prophet Muhammad and go with him to Muslim heavens. Some children would converse with Buddha or with Krishna, Rama, or Hindu gods. Many of the children just experienced a great and overwhelming peace, a bright light that illuminated their whole day. They would discover an intelligence that would guide them and tell them all they needed to know. The director explained to them in the spiritual classes that this was called the *antaryamin,* the indweller in the heart that guides all beings toward greater truth.

Many children found that they could travel outside their physical bodies. They could just lie down and visit their homes and see what their families were doing. Later, when their parents came to the school to collect them for vacation, the children would run out: "Mother, Father, I saw you three days ago. Mother, you were wearing your yellow dress. Father, you were talking to your friend from Delhi on the phone; you were telling him about the job you wanted." The parents would ask, "How do you know all this?" And the children would say, "I was there." This became quite commonplace after a while, like any normal talk.

The children would go into states of great joy for no reason at all and discover tremendous love for one another, for the animals, for the plants. None of this was taught to them; it came from within. Healing became a common occurrence at the school; children found out how they could heal each other. Giri recalls:

Children would heal themselves of all kinds of diseases. Nobody wore glasses. If a child used to wear glasses, someone touched him and he was healed. For three years, we never had a doctor on the campus. So many amazing things were happening. We used to move into other dimensions, lie down, and touch the stars.

Krishna and Giri would get up before dawn, jump on their bikes, and take off for the big rocks on the outer part of the campus. There they would lie on their backs, spread out under the stars, and find themselves transported into other dimensions. They would have visions of the school director and his wife as divine beings. Sometimes they would appear in a golden form; sometimes, surrounded by other golden beings. When the visions dissolved, Krishna and Giri would open their eyes and whisper to each other what they had each seen. It was always the same vision for both of them. As time went by, many of the other children had similar visions of the director and his wife and came to regard them with new eyes. They started to refer to the school director as Sri Bhagavan, which roughly translates to Holy One, and to his wife as Sri Amma, or Divine Mother. These names have stayed with them to this day.

Krishna had always felt that his father was different from the parents of the other boys. Now these visions confirmed it was true. True to his word, he reported all these things to his father.

"Now we are seeing you and Mother in our hearts, and you seem to be golden, too," Krishna reported to his father one day. "Who are you, Father? I know you are not like other men." Bhagavan looked for a long time at his son without speaking. By the time he did speak, Krishna could already feel in his heart what his father was about to say.

"We are both avatars, Krishna. It simply means that we were born to help humanity. We have a work to do in the world. A big change is needed on the Earth at this time, in the hearts of all people. You will see; you will also play a big part in this, and so will Giri and many others who are here."

• • •

Bhagavan was born in Nattham, a small village in Tamil Nadu, in March 1949. He describes the circumstances of his birth:

My mother was a very innocent woman from a village. In Indian tradition, they believe that it is possible for God to be born to them as their child. She was thirteen years old when she got married. She used to go to the temple and worship Krishna there, saying, "You must be born to me as my child." She used to see God as baby Krishna within her. Krishna would also speak to her from within, and she was feeling that he was the one who was going to be born to her. When she gave birth, Krishna's form disappeared within her. Maybe that influenced me. I do not know. But from as early as I can remember, I could feel that people around me were not experiencing what I was experiencing. I was always wondering, "How am I to give it to them?" Then I realized it has to be actually transferred to them. So this work began when I was a child.

Bhagavan's father was the head of the accounts department for the local railways. He also had a small farm in the village of Nemam, not far from the state capital of Madras. When Bhagavan was six years old, the family moved to Madras.

My father was an atheist, a no-nonsense person. I spent most of my time by myself. He used to ask me, "What do you propose to do with your life?" I said, "I'm going to transform the world." Then he would ask, "What do you think you are?" and I used to tell him, "I am God." That put real fear into him. The family got together wondering whether they should take me to a psychiatrist—maybe I was suffering from a Messiah complex. But they found I was quite ordinary otherwise. I was good at academics. I was doing my work and was causing no trouble to others. He put up with this for many, many years. He used to ask me, "What do you propose to do?" And the same answer would come out.

I often say that I am God. It has to be carefully understood. To me, all life is one. There is only one life. It is that which is flowing through you, through me, through the lion, the elephant, the tiger, the ant, through the trees, the sun and the moon and the universe. The same one life is expressing itself through all these forms, and that life is what I call God. So I am God, you are God, the ant is God, the elephant is God, the one in prison is God, the crook is God, the saint is God, and the sage is God. These are the different manifestations of God. God has become all this. He is not different from creation. It is like the spider that brings out the web from its own body. It is God who has become all this.

The experience of God is a real experience, within the realm of possibility for all people. It is not fiction; it is not philosophical speculation. This is something that can be your day-to-day living experience. It is where the deekshas should ultimately take you. Then you can boldly say, "I am God." That is why I take the stand that I am God. It has been my feeling ever since childhood.

From childhood, Bhagavan realized that the way he was experiencing the world was not the same way other people experienced it. Before recognizing this, he did not think of himself as an avatar; he simply thought that his experience was normal.

I watched the way people behaved, and I wondered why they acted that way. Ever since I was born, I could experience what other people were experiencing. I found that their reality was very different from mine. When I feel the world, I listen to some sound, and I find that I'm not interpreting it. When I look at something, again there is no interpretation going on. There is nobody who is hearing, nobody who is seeing. There is nobody there; there's just the experience of the seeing, the hearing, the thinking. When I allowed myself to experience what other people experience, I found that they had the feeling that somebody was there doing these things. It has never been like that for me. I had to experience others to know how they were relating to the world. I never went through any process of enlightenment, because it was there all the time from the beginning.

So I decided something had to be done there. When I was experiencing, I was getting joy. I found others were getting no joy at all. I realized that the idea of somebody being there has to go. That is how it all began.

The young Bhagavan attended the Don Bosco School in Madras, where he was educated by Jesuit priests and graduated in mathematics. He excelled academically, despite the fact that he had very little attention available for his studies. Throughout his childhood, he felt compelled by a higher power—something that he did not understand—to chant certain mantras and to hold his body in certain postures. A huge golden ball would appear to him a great deal of the time. None of these things happened by his volition. In fact, very often, he wanted to go and play with his friends, to join their cricket or football matches, but he recounts that he felt compelled, held captive almost, by this higher power, which commanded him to perform all kinds of spiritual practices. It was not until the same golden ball descended into Mathew and named itself all those years later that he understood the significance of his childhood visions.

His father continued to ask Bhagavan, even into his twenties, what he planned to do with his life, and he always got the same answer: "I plan to change the world." And so it was decided that the best thing would be for the boy to marry. That would give him some sense of worldly responsibility and duty. The young Bhagavan always did everything he could to make his parents happy, and he willingly agreed to the plan. As is customary in India, his parents conducted a search and found a suitable bride in the nearby village of Sangam. Some mutual family friends arranged a meeting of the two, and within the first seconds, there was a profound and mutual recognition.

Amma, who was born as Padmavati, also had an unusual childhood. She used to rise very early in the morning, go to the river near her house, and pray and perform rituals to the divine that she made up herself. Her only obsession was that she wanted to marry God. The other girls were interested in clothes or boys or movies, but she stayed focused on this one thing. This sole passion in her, even as a young child, led her to be revered as an incarnation of the

Divine Mother by the local saints and elders. Today, all the rituals that Amma devised by the riverbanks have been carried on by local girls in the village, hoping to magnetize such a great match in a husband.

Bhagavan continues the story:

My father continued to ask me, "Who do you think you are?" and I never changed my answer: "I am God." So finally, once I was in my twenties, he said, "This is really too much." That was when he organized my marriage, and I willingly agreed. The marriage took place, but then the same thing continued. It was worse now, because I was still saying, "I am God," and now my wife was saying, "I prayed to marry God, and now I am God's wife!" With his strong atheistic background, my father could not take this anymore. Finally, he came to me one day and said, "If it is all true, convince me. Show me that it is true; give me some kind of experience." I said, "I will do that." He had a lot of mystical experiences. He became very happy. A few months later, he died—he died of sheer happiness.

Soon after the wedding, Amma and Bhagavan began to make plans to open a school. From the beginning, Amma was a central part of its formation.

• • •

By 1991, the school was fully transformed. Academic studies continued, but just like for the young Bhagavan, they were now a secondary preoccupation for the children as well as for the teachers. Everyone was absorbed in deep mystical experiences: of different deities, of profound silence and deep causeless joy and love. People would smell all kinds of sacred smells, like incense, for no reason. People would hear chanting in different languages, as though a choir of angels had descended. Even people passing on the road outside or making deliveries to the campus would have these experiences.

There was a mixed reaction to all this from the parents of the children. Some were very pleased—so pleased, in fact, that they demanded to have the same visions as their children. But others complained, saying, "We sent our children here to become doctors, lawyers, and accountants, not mystics. What are you doing to them?" Out of all this, Bhagavan made a simple decision—to slowly wind down the school and open a center for the spiritual work. Within a few weeks, the mystical experiences within the children became much less frequent, and the first retreat was offered for the parents. Jyoti remembers her meeting with Bhagavan at that time:

My parents were very afraid. I didn't want to take my tenth standard exams. I wanted to stop my studies, stay back with Amma and Bhagavan and be part of the spiritual work that was beginning. Our first intensive had happened, and I wanted to join this work. I knew it was a lot for me to ask. Bhagavan said to me, "Now your battle begins. You have to become fully functional." He said, "Sit in front of me." I sat. He said, "Keep your eyes open." After fifteen minutes or so, when I stood up, I felt I was ready to handle anything. The peak state that had been there was gone. The intensity of that experience was gone. Then began my battles: I had to go home and convince my parents. They wouldn't agree. I took my tenth standard exams anyway, as studies were no longer difficult. It was very easy. There was so much attention. Amma and Bhagavan always made us feel that education was very easy. The worry was gone. To learn anything is not difficult.

After she completed her education, Jyoti went home to live with her family and could only visit the school occasionally. It took three years for her family to agree to her participating in the work that was unfolding. When she finally did return, she was given the name Samadarshini. Today, she is one of the three senior teachers, or *acharyas,* of the Oneness University.

It took three more years for Jeevashram to wind down completely. Bhagavan insisted that all the children be allowed to finish their education, so the most junior class had to move through to graduation. But at the same time, the spiritual courses began. The first courses held at the school were for parents, but soon a second campus, named Somangalam, was opened much closer to Madras. The principal moved there with a small group from the school who were now teenagers. Giri became Anandagiri, and Satish became Vimalkirti. They are now the university's other two acharyas.

Courses were offered for three, six, and ten days. The focus was primarily on creating a suitable foundation for the full awakening of consciousness: setting right relationships, healing the body, and developing the capacity to feel the emotional hurt that had been repressed and to feel the hurt that had been caused to others. The emphasis was always on direct experience, on a shift in the brain. Hence, there was very little in the way of teachings or spiritual practices: the central part of the courses was always the deeksha. Participants would come to recognize the ways they had left their relationships unresolved, their pain unfelt, and to see their own powerlessness to do anything about it. They would be encouraged to reach out for divine help. Then Krishna, Anandagiri, and the other boys—just teenagers—would give the deekshas, and the participants would experience miraculous healings in every dimension of their lives. All the courses at that time were offered for free, though some participants made donations. Almost everyone attending was Indian. A young Swedish boy traveling in India was one of the few Westerners who attended those early courses. He recalls:

> I went to the first full-one-week course. There was no teaching, only Anandagiri and Krishna transferring some special energies. I was filled with light, completely calmed, and then there followed a flood of revelations and insights, all on their own. The principal from the school led the course, but all the deekshas were given by these young boys: thirteen, fourteen, fifteen. I had traveled in India, and I had met many people who were enlightened, including Ammachi and the teachers I met at Ramana Ashram. They had all made a very big impression on me. But somehow my heart was even more touched by these children. I just cried; I couldn't stop my tears from flowing. They had such divine innocence and beauty—it was like a fairy tale. I went back to Ramana Ashram. They had told me, "You can do different

meditations now. You can ask the divine presence inside to help you.
You can ask for any spiritual experience." My mind became detached,
in a state of immense peace. After that course, everything else I tried
just worked.

• • •

By the summer of 1994, the last batch of students graduated from the school, and it was officially closed. The campus was renamed Satyaloka, and the young acharyas returned there. Demand was growing from all over India for the extraordinary gift that these teenagers could bring with a simple touch on the head. Bhagavan's sister and her husband had hosted the first public meeting in Madras in 1993. Thereafter, invitations flew in from everywhere. The teenagers began to travel all over India, offering courses, and Amma and Bhagavan effectively retired from the public eye. They moved to a private house near the beach in Madras, where they lived quietly, taking walks and enjoying each other's company. Once a month or so, they would meet with the band of young acharyas, feel satisfied that all was going well, and then return to their seclusion. It went on like this for nearly four years.

Soon it became apparent that there were not nearly enough teachers to go around, and a decision was made to start an order of dasas, otherwise known as guides. Young men and women joined. Some were the children of families who had already experienced deeksha, but many were teenagers who had powerful visions, all on their own, of a calling for their lives to serve the spiritual transformation of humanity. They might have had a vision of Amma or Bhagavan, or they might have been called to go to a certain place at a certain time and thus meet with the young acharyas.

Many of the Indian youth who joined at that time have fascinating stories to tell. The order of dasas had none of the rules that are common to a monastic order. They could eat as they liked, dress as they liked, and they were free to leave the order at any time with honor. It was from within themselves that they slowly came to agree on some ways to be together. No rule was ever imposed upon them from the outside.

During those years, hundreds of thousands of people in India received deekshas from the acharyas, and then from the dasas, without ever seeing Amma or Bhagavan in person. They had to rely upon an inner connection, and that inner connection grew. At that time, Amma was hardly known, at her request; all the focus was on Bhagavan as the source of the deeksha phenomenon. Then a few people in northern India got hold of a copy of her picture, which had been taken at the school. Stories began to spread of miraculous healings in connection with that picture—relationships being healed, financial problems turning around. She developed a reputation as an emanation of the Divine Mother, although people did not know who she was or even that she was married.

Today, Amma and Bhagavan are widely recognized in India as twin emanations of the same avataric consciousness. Amma explains it like this:

Amma and Bhagavan are one. They are the mother and the father aspect of the divine. Bhagavan gives people grace as the father; Amma, as the mother, fulfills their desires, needs, health problems—in fact, everything. Bhagavan is always concerned with the spiritual growth of people and leading people toward mukti—liberation—while Amma is immersed in fulfilling people's desires.

Even with Amma and Bhagavan in seclusion, the work continued to spread like wildfire all over India. In March of 1997, around the time of Bhagavan's birthday, which has always involved a big celebration, there were a hundred different events organized all over Madras, where the young dasas gave talks and deekshas. Each event attracted big crowds, and it came to the attention of the local government. When they saw many young people gathering, the only thing they could think of was the possibility of a new political party emerging and thus a threat to their power. Stories circulated on television of abductions of minors, even of violence or murder within the headquarters at Satyaloka. The police came, but none of these rumors was ever substantiated. It was, however, enough to create tremendous public fear. At the same time, the government created the rumor that Amma and Bhagavan did not actually exist, that they were fictitious figureheads for an anarchist political party created by the young dasas.

It was to dispel these rumors that Amma and Bhagavan were pulled out of their seclusion and back into public life. That spring, they met with the dasas, who had grown to a body of more than a hundred, on the lawn behind their old house at Satyaloka. A public *darshan** was announced for May. One hundred and fifty thousand people attended from all over India. People waited in lines miles long to be able to see, face to face, the avatars they had only previously seen in pictures.

Once Amma and Bhagavan returned to making regular public appearances, their work and reputation grew even more. A second center was opened in Nemam, on the site of the farm that had belonged to Bhagavan's father, purely for Amma's public appearances, which, to this day, attract ten thousand people or more each day. At the same time, a small number of Westerners began to hear about the phenomenon that had, to this point, been primarily Indian. The first course purely for Western guests took place in 1998, with forty participants from Russia, the United States, and Scandinavia.

Things grew at a faster rate every year, and it became clear that even the two-hundred-acre campus at Satyaloka was not big enough to house the increasing number of guests. An exhaustive search began for the right place. Krishna, now nearly twenty, traveled more than fifty thousand miles a year for several years, looking for a suitable and large enough parcel of land. One day in 1999, Anandagiri, together with the other dasas, was finishing a forty-day international retreat at Satyaloka when he received a call from Krishna. "I think you should come right away," Krishna said. "I have found something very special. Come now. I will meet you at Varadaiahpalem." As we will hear later, Varadaiahpalem at that time was one of the most run-down and unattractive places in southern India. It was infamous for drinking, spousal abuse, fighting, and severe unemployment. Krishna's call was like an invitation to visit the South Bronx. But Anandagiri went.

Krishna took Anandagiri to an extraordinary place for sale, nestled in the middle of government forest land. With its waterfall and creeks, it was like a scene from paradise. They both knew they had found it. The land had

---

*darshan—literally sight, vision, or glimpse. It is commonly used to mean a vision of the divine or a very holy person.

been inherited by some brothers, with the stipulation in their father's will that it could only be sold to a spiritual group for work that would benefit humanity. Krishna and Anandagiri took this as the sign they had been waiting for. Money was donated, and the land was purchased. Over the following months, more parcels were bought from different owners. This land now houses the Oneness University, which includes eleven sprawling campuses and one of India's largest temples, which is dedicated to Oneness rather than to any specific deity. It is also the headquarters of social projects to revitalize more than 140 local communities, affecting more than 100,000 people. We will hear much more about all these things later in this book.

Bhagavan and the dasas moved to the first campus, completed in the year 2000. The move allowed not only a shift of location but also a dramatic shift in consciousness. Bhagavan had always talked of enlightenment as a specific state of brain functioning, as the natural state of human consciousness; bringing people fully into this state of brain functioning now became the primary focus of the university's work. All the dasas, now numbering 170, went through an intensive course of preparation and deekshas, and all of them passed a threshold in brain consciousness that Bhagavan calls Awakening into Oneness. The university began to offer "*mukti* courses" of graduated degrees of intensity, aimed primarily at catapulting participants into awakening consciousness.

In January 2004, the university offered its first twenty-one-day course for Westerners, the program for which it is now best known all over the world. This course is required before one is able to give the Oneness Blessing. Now known as the Oneness Process, the course takes place on a specially designed campus, just across the road from the Oneness Temple. Each month, several hundred visitors from all over the world come to the Oneness University to undergo an intensive process, during which participants are in silence for most of the time. The course is constantly evolving, redesigned fresh each time by the dasas themselves in response to the experiences of recent course participants and graduates from all over the world. You will read much more about the experiences people have had in the Oneness Process in the last chapter.

Over the past few years, more than twelve thousand people all over the world have been initiated to give the Oneness Blessing in more than fifty countries. They include psychotherapists, doctors, writers, actors, Christian bishops, Muslim imams, Jewish rabbis, Hindu sadhus, indigenous shamans, and everyone in between. It is estimated that tens of millions of people have now received this blessing, and the number is growing every day. What is it about this phenomenon that has ignited the hearts of so many people, from so many diverse backgrounds, in so short a time? To answer this question, we need to get a deeper understanding of the phenomenon itself and what it does to the brain and nervous system.

CHAPTER THREE

WHAT IS THE
ONENESS BLESSING?

T ake one step toward God," my grandmother used to tell me, "and God will take a hundred steps toward you." I was never quite sure how to begin. Prayer, ritual, meditation—these are all ways we have found, over millennia, to take a step toward the divine. This endless thirst to know God has spawned our religious fervor, as well as the greater part of our poetry, music, architecture, literature, and mythology.

The Oneness Blessing, on the other hand, is one way that the divine can take a hundred steps toward us. The Blessing affects the brain in such a way that we can be touched by grace. It puts us in touch with benediction, with the source of all that we have always longed for. It is a gift.

The Oneness Blessing appears to be transferred from one person to another, but that, according to Bhagavan, is only the appearance of it. "Deeksha is the phenomenon wherein the divine reaches out to man," he says. "The person who is giving the deeksha is making himself or herself available to the divine and becomes an instrument. There's literally no role for the personal dimension. It depends upon how the divine wants to make use of that person; he or she merely becomes a conduit for it."

After attending the twenty-one-day Oneness Process in India, graduates are able to give the Blessing to others. But it is not a skill that is learned or something one gets good at. During the course, one is simply washed clean of oneself through experiencing and letting go of things that have been held from the past. After enough preparation, the Blessing can come through the one giving it; the giver has simply discovered how to be still and step out of the way. The grace that flows through the Blessing is timeless. We have all been touched by grace at one time or another in our lives, so this is not something new. Sometimes we recognize it, and sometimes we don't. The Oneness Blessing is that same grace but with a tremendous focus and intent. It has direction and divine intelligence. It is the force of the divine, awakening humanity to our full potential—the next evolutionary leap we must now take together in order to enter the next phase of being alive.

This Blessing can come through the person giving it in several ways. The most common way is through touch, known in India as *sparsha deeksha*. The Blessing giver places his or her hands on the receiver's head for one or two minutes. It can also be given through the eyes, which is called *nayana deeksha*. Here, the Blessing giver looks into the receiver's eyes for several minutes. Finally, it can be given through intention, referred to as *smarana deeksha*. In this case, the Blessing giver holds the receiver in his or her awareness for a few minutes and allows the Blessing to be given. In this way, the Blessing can be given at a distance of thousands of miles or to a large group of people all at the same time.

WHAT IS IT LIKE TO RECEIVE THE ONENESS BLESSING?

Receiving the Oneness Blessing can be experienced in all kinds of ways. We could call them the good, the bad, and the nothing at all. Ultimately, our subjective experience of the Blessing is fleeting, and the changes in the brain that are described in the next chapter will happen regardless of how we experience it.

Some people, but by no means all, have extremely pleasant experiences of the Blessing. Here, Lindsay Wagner (well known in the 1970s as the "Bionic Woman") describes her first two experiences, one of which was given through the eyes, and one through the head:

> *Everything disappeared. There was no my body; there was no his body; there was just a perception of his eye and my eye. Then there was nothing, and that was it. I started to smile and to laugh. Eventually, the rest of the room and the normal perception of me and him in the room came back. Later, he put his hands on my head to give*

me the Blessing. I closed my eyes and went and lay down. While I was lying there, there was a low hum, like an engine running. I felt it throughout my whole body. It was like after you do a lot of mental work and then sit down and just relax. I felt the energy calming down in my head and opening up in the other parts of my body. At one point, I felt some grief moving through. I started crying. Then it was gone. The whole experience was like when you are in love. You are not with your beloved, but you sit somewhere and think of him. It felt like that. There was nothing; there was no desire for anything. There was no angst about anything. There was no fear. There was just this sweet state of existing, feeling peaceful, feeling that "it's just good to be alive." Later, things were really funny. Food that normally tastes good tasted really good, like my senses were much more alive, and so was my state of peace. It was warmer and deeper.

Not everyone, however, feels good during such a Blessing. It could just as well release difficult feelings that we have been unwilling to experience previously and that have been stuck in the body. The interesting thing is that although a significant number of people subjectively experience the Blessing in this way, they still recognize it as a positive experience.

Rick Allen is the one-armed drummer of the heavy metal band Def Leppard. In 1984, at the peak of the band's popularity, Rick was involved in a horrible car accident just outside his hometown in northern England. While attempting to pass another car on a curve, he lost control, and the car rolled over down a steep hill. The seat belt came undone and caught his arm. Rick was thrown a hundred yards into a field; his arm stayed in the car, along with his girlfriend. Rick was in the hospital for six months, and the doctors told him he would never play drums again. That gave him the motivation he needed to prove them wrong. He had a special drum kit created that used both feet and his one remaining arm, and in less than a year, the band was performing again. The determination Rick mustered to rise above his challenge never really allowed him to fully experience the trauma of the accident. Here is Rick's first experience of a Oneness Blessing:

I don't have a nice story to tell you. I was really angry afterward. It whacked the beehive; it really stirred a lot up in me. During the Blessing, I started seeing colors—throbbing purples and blues—then all kinds of images started to appear. Quite quickly, we got up to leave. On the way home in the car, I started to feel a lot of anger. I was ranting and raving a bit, then I pulled over. I didn't know what was going on. There must have been a lot of things in me that were residual from my life experiences. I felt confusion and frustration. I remember punching the center of the steering wheel. I had a familiar feeling of information overload; I couldn't even think. I felt imprisoned. There were no weird and wonderful stories to go along with this. It was literally just experiencing rage in my body. They say that the body remembers everything. I think it unlocked some things that night.

This initiated a deeper process for Rick, which was equally uncomfortable until things opened up:

I knew there was something more than what I was going through in my life: the frustrations that I experienced on a daily basis, trying to control everything around me. I started to realize that I'm not in the driver's seat here. Then something shifted. After the first few Blessings, I started to feel joy for no particular reason. I started to feel full. I could look at anything and just start to enjoy it. I started having conversations with ant colonies and just really feeling connected to everything.

The interesting thing about Rick's story—and the stories of many others—is that although his subjective experience was not comfortable, he continued to receive more such Blessings. Just like taking a homeopathic remedy that might make you feel quite awful for a while and provoke a healing crisis, some deeper intuition in us knows that the Oneness Blessing is leading us in the direction of healing.

Catherine Oxenberg is best known for her role in *Dynasty* and for her portrayal of Lady Diana Spencer in the TV miniseries *The Royal Romance of*

Charles and Diana. She was spending the weekend in San Francisco with her family when Marci Shimoff, her hostess, invited them to a Oneness Blessing event in Santa Cruz.

I was skeptical, cynical, and disinterested, but we went to Santa Cruz anyway. I dragged my husband, and he drove, with my eldest daughter, who was thirteen at the time. We sat there in a group of aging hippies. We arrived late and left early. Marci felt something immediately. I was jealous because I felt nothing. People were having all kinds of experiences in the room, and we were laughing at them; my daughter was mortified that we were behaving so badly. We left the program, and we were driving back in the car, and that's when I noticed a shift. My husband was talking; what he was saying would have normally really annoyed me. I would have reacted to it, and I would have felt that feeling in my gut, that reactive place in my body. Instead, everything that came out of his mouth felt like bubbles of joy in my body. I realized that I was actually experiencing him, maybe for the first time, without reacting to him. There was nothing during the event that gave me any indication that any shift was occurring at all. Nothing. But later, I realized I had experienced a profound shift in consciousness without even realizing it.

Catherine realized on the way home in the car that something had shifted. For some, it may take days or even weeks or months to notice that a change has gradually crept up on them.

Bhagavan explains that ultimately the subjective nature of our experience during the deeksha, or Blessing, is unimportant. As we will see later, the changes that the Blessing brings about in the brain happen anyway, no matter what our experience feels like. He explains that there are three factors that contribute to why we feel a certain way:

One is the person receiving the deeksha, another is the person giving the deeksha, and the third is the divine itself. It depends upon how

receptive you are, what your beliefs are, and what your conditioning is.
Even so, we have noticed that sometimes people who we thought would
make very little progress are making dramatic progress. We have seen in-
stances of people sleeping through courses and still becoming awakened.
We have had people one might call immoral, people one might think
are not the right kind of people to receive deeksha. But they end up as
the most transformed people. It also depends on the person who is giving
the deeksha. And then there's the divine, of course, which is the ultimate
source of all this. Whatever the divine decides, it happens.

OVERALL TRENDS

While subjective experiences may differ from one person to another, as
well as in the same person from one Blessing to the next, the millions of
people all over the world who have received the Oneness Blessing allow us
to discover certain overall trends. These generalized experiences may occur
during and immediately following the Blessing itself. They may also accu-
mulate over many months of receiving many Blessings. All these changes
can be explained by the effects of the Oneness Blessing on the brain, which
will be covered in the next chapter. These effects include the following:

Reduced Mind Chatter and Heightened Sensory Awareness

Both during the Blessing and for three to four hours following, it is normal
to experience a quieting of mental activity. With repeated Blessings, this spills
over into daily life. Colors become brighter; tastes and smells are more vivid;
things become more interesting. Rani Kumra, who lives in the San Francisco
Bay Area, was one of the first Americans to receive the Oneness training, and
she has since given it to thousands of people. She says:

The mind is unclogged, your senses are heightened, and the sense of sepa-
ration decreases. Your perception changes about everything. Problems
may still exist, but they may not seem like problems anymore, because
now you're perceiving the same thing from a different angle. Previously,

the mind was chattering; you were judging others and judging yourself. Now you perceive it totally differently. There is no conflict within the mind at all, so all the energy is in whatever you're doing.

Effortless Feeling of Peace and Comfort

In terms of the shift it induces, the Oneness Blessing has sometimes been compared to various kinds of meditation and other spiritual practices. But many people with decades of experience with meditation practices maintain that the Oneness Blessing has been quite a departure for them. Here is Rani Kumra again:

In meditation, you may experience peace when you meditate; the brain may go into silence. But after you get up, as you go into your routine work, you go back into the conflict of the mind. You go back into suffering.

Ralf Franziskowski is a medical doctor in Traunstein, Germany. As a specialist in natural medicine and psychotherapy, he has spent decades practicing meditation on longer retreats and as part of his daily routine.

I had glimpses of being one, not separate, as a result of my meditation practice. But it crossed over very little into my daily life, where I continued to feel very separate from everything. I felt very sad about this split. Since receiving the Oneness Blessing, and especially since going to India and learning to give the Blessing, this split has become less and less. In meditation, I would come to a point where fear would take over. Then I would retreat and say, "No, I don't want to go any further." It would get hard to feel what was in my body. This fear has now gone, replaced by a natural sense of freedom. In my daily life, I'm more connected with the sense of oneness that I knew from my meditation practice.

Diminishing Inner Conflict

One of the most common reports from people regularly receiving Blessings is that things flow more smoothly in life, that there is less need to make decisions, and that things happen easily on their own. Maneesh de Moor, a Dutch musician, told me, "I feel like I am flowing through life now, rather than being stuck somewhere. The river is flowing; I'm flowing with it, without getting blocked here and blocked there." Anandagiri, one of the three acharyas at the Oneness University, says:

> It becomes obvious after a while that this is not a change in thinking—it is a clear change in the way that you are experiencing things. It is not a practice that you have cultivated or a new ideology. People feel really comfortable with themselves. They do not complain about who they are. There is a sense of deep peace and comfort inside one's self—a lack of inner conflict.

Becoming an Observer

We are habituated to becoming fully identified with our thoughts and feelings. When a wave of anger arises, we feel, "I am angry," rather than notice the wave of anger rising, passing through, and dissipating again. Hence, we become a slave to that anger. It rules us, and we lose the possibility of any choice about it. The same is true of our beliefs. We defend them as if our lives depend on them. People receiving the Oneness Blessing report that this habit gets quite quickly broken, that shifts in the brain allow us to experience our thoughts and feelings with dispassion. Here is Rick Allen again:

> I guess the most noticeable thing is the ability to be an observer. Instead of being in the sticky stuff, you're able to kind of get out of yourself and just see yourself almost like another person. It's quite useful, because in whatever situation you're in, you tend not to get flustered. There's less likelihood of allowing your emotions to rule your world. It's great when you do it as a couple, because you remind each other. You go, "There's no point in getting all upset about that. It's okay." It was subtle at first, but it really starts to come on strong, in all kinds of situations.

Breaking of Patterns

Many people report that in addition to being able to observe their habitual thoughts and feelings without being governed by them, those patterns themselves begin to naturally dissipate and melt away. Of the hundreds of people interviewed for this book, many reported that they would suddenly notice, in retrospect, that a habit had not shown itself for some time. This had required no effort or decision on their part; it just disappeared on its own. Here is Samadarshini, another acharya at the Oneness University:

We are used to going in circles, thinking the same thing again and again. I've seen deeksha break this. People say, "My God, my obsession is gone." The deeksha allows you to see that your obsession was only an obsession, and then it changes. It had nothing real to it. I've seen people become extremely happy. So happy that addictions are no longer required. They drop away. In the university, we never tell people to give up any addiction. We don't tell anyone to do anything. Things change because people are so happy. Something happens to their brain whereby they don't seem to need these things anymore. They have gotten over it. They don't seem to need pain, either. So many times pain defines our life. Suffering defines our life. People don't seem to need any suffering or pain. It's gone.

Peak Experiences

The changes we have described so far all concern our usual, day-to-day life becoming better—more comfortable, less stressed, and more functional. While these changes are real, and entirely welcome for the beneficiaries, people frequently report another kind of result altogether. The changes we have described so far could be said to be changes in the person. It is also very common, especially during longer Oneness courses, for there to be a dissolving of the sense of a separate person completely—an Awakening into Oneness. We will return to this topic in much greater depth in a later chapter. Here is Sri Bhagavan:

We believe that ultimately deeksha leads to what we call Oneness. You lose the sense of separation. People feel as though they all belong to the same family. We believe the world will become one global family. We see that as the ultimate happening.

INTENTION

So far we have described the effects of the Oneness Blessing as a universal panacea that will reduce stress and bring us to a feeling of Oneness. At the same time, an evolutionary or healing intention can be applied when giving the Blessing to give the process a direction. Known as a *sankalpa* at the Oneness University, the intention—of the giver, the receiver, and ultimately divine intelligence itself—will determine the effect of each Oneness Blessing. Hence, the Blessing has been used as a powerful tool for physical healing, for restoring financial well-being, for resolving problems in relationships, and for creating a host of other practical outcomes.

Sankalpa has no precise translation in English, so let's just use the Sanskrit word. Bhagavan explains it like this:

You look at a person who is very sick, and you feel touched; you want to help him out. A strong desire is born. If the person who is receiving the deeksha also has the same intent, it becomes doubly powerful. To have strong sankalpa, the heart has to flower; you have to listen to the other person and really feel for him. If somebody else comes and tells you about her financial problems, you must put yourself in her shoes, see her suffering and her wants. Then you begin to empathize with her. Finally, you give the deeksha. You must take your time, listen to the person, meet his or her family, begin to feel for that person—and then give the deeksha. You must feel from the heart. The heart plays a key role. If you take it into your head without warmth in the heart, then deeksha is not going to be really effective.

Bhagavan continues to explain that the expertise and confidence of a Oneness Blessing giver in a particular area of life will greatly increase the chances of the Blessing's being effective. So a medical practitioner giving the Oneness

Blessing will be most effective for physical healing. The Blessing from a financial wizard like Tony Robbins—who is a trained Blessing giver—can help set your money worries straight. Ultimately, the Blessing from someone stably resting in the realization of Oneness will most rapidly accelerate spiritual maturity. Here is Bhagavan again:

> *Deeksha for healing a heart complaint, for example, would be most effective if the giver also happens to be a medical doctor. The first thing is that he has to feel compelled to help this person. The second thing is that he must have a picture of what is going on within the heart. Now, with that knowledge, he can have the sankalpa of the arteries getting opened up. When he gives the deeksha, then, the arteries may well in fact open.*

For this reason, the vision at the Oneness University is to have specialist Oneness Blessing givers, each confident and proficient in a specific arena of life and able to give strong sankalpa in that area.

It is not always necessary that the recipient of the Blessing even know what is occurring. In just the same way that we can pray for someone's well-being or physical healing without his or her knowledge, we can give a Blessing on others' behalf. When I returned from my first visit to the Oneness University, the last leg of my journey home was from San Francisco to Sacramento—a forty-minute hop. The plane had been delayed by three or four hours. There was a German woman sitting just behind me, on the other side of the aisle, who had been traveling all the way from Germany. She was jet-lagged and frustrated. As our plane started to move toward the runway, she looked out the window and saw her suitcase still on a luggage trolley with many other bags. She started to scream, "My suitcase, my suitcase, it is still there, we must go back." The flight attendant reassured the woman that another plane would be leaving in a few minutes and that it would bring all the luggage. But the woman was very overtired and became more and more hysterical. "No, no!" she screamed. "Stop the plane right now!" The other passengers tried to console her, but nothing helped. I closed my eyes and felt her anxiety with her, her longing for things to be all right, to be safe. I gave her the Oneness Blessing with this sankalpa of trust, and in a few minutes, she was sleeping like a baby. Was it the Blessing or sheer exhaustion that put her to sleep? We will never know.

At the Oneness University in India, Bhagavan and his wife, Amma, often give strong sankalpas themselves: sometimes for a specific person, sometimes for a group of people, and sometimes for the whole campus of ten thousand people or more. Samadarshini recalls one such time:

> I have noticed that deeksha flows according to the intent of Bhagavan. Whatever Amma and Bhagavan decide, that is what happens in the deeksha here in the university. It is given a direction by them. That has been my experience over the past seventeen years now. They also give deekshas for the dasas. When their intent is that silence happens to us, silence happens. The other day Bhagavan said, "I want an explosion of joy in the dasas." That's what happened. The entire campus shook with our joy. It was an explosion. The divine power is always there, but it is given direction by them, by their intent.

When we Westerners hear stories like this, some of us might feel quite afraid that we are being taken over by mind control, that we are losing our free will. In our culture, we have glorified individual willpower; to interfere with another person is the greatest taboo. America's theme song is Frank Sinatra's *I Did It My Way.* Although our culture may be fully immersed in this supremacy of the individual will, it has not always been this way—and it is not this way in every culture even today. Almost every spiritual tradition has recognized that surrender to divine will, or to a wise guide, may be a much saner way to live. "Wash me clean of myself," says Rumi. "Not my will, but Thy will be done," says St. Thomas Aquinas.

Ultimately, it is divine will itself that will determine the outcome of the Oneness Blessing. Someone may have the intention for more money, and that person may ask the Blessing giver to have the intention for more money. But when the Blessing is given, the receiver may experience all kinds of memories and feelings about his or her father. This has happened many times. The One-ness Blessing has its own intelligence and knows what to do and where to go for the recipient's greatest well-being.

CHAPTER FOUR

THE ONENESS BLESSING AND THE BRAIN

Perhaps the most controversial claim of the Oneness University—at least for people with a background in spiritual practice—is that spiritual awakening is primarily a neurobiological process. So many of us have put great faith in teachings, in gaining fresh understanding, in changing habits and beliefs, in asking ourselves the right kinds of questions, in trying to remain vigilant. Almost no attention is given to these things at the university. Often, Oneness Blessings are given for a specific sankalpa with virtually no explanation at all. The dasas report that the changes in the brain that support awakening happen more easily without the conscious participation of the recipient; our attempts to become more awakened may be more of a hindrance than a help. Here is Anandagiri:

The way we experience what surrounds us, the way we relate to ourselves, to the people around us, to the things around us, the way we respond to situations, all depends on how our brain is functioning. As the balance of brain activity changes, the sense of separation begins to slowly disappear. You begin to feel more and more connected to people, closer to people, connected to everything around you. You really feel one with everything. You feel more and more joy, more and more love. The way you relate to your everyday experiences, the simple things of everyday life, is affected. So it should be possible to start mapping the changes in the brain and then start studying the change in the behavior of the person. And I would expect that they correlate perfectly. If all of this is governed by the state of the brain, what does it matter which teaching you subscribe to, or which faith you follow? It is totally immaterial.

Before we go any further with this chapter, it feels important to interject that I am not a scientist. The last biology class I took at school was when I was fifteen. I got a C. The only thing I learned then about the brain was that it is gray, lives inside your scalp, and can be quite useful for getting things done. A reputable scientist might advise me to not touch the subject at all; in fact, a few already have. The reason to include something about the brain here is that so much of the conversation about the Oneness Blessing has been speculation about its potential effect on the brain—to write about this phenomenon without mentioning this speculation would be something like writing about Italy and not mentioning food or wine just because one does not cook. In order to write about this topic, I interviewed dozens of people with anything interesting to say about the subject. Some were practitioners in conventional or alternative medicine, and some were psychologists who had notions about what was happening in the brain, based upon their clinical observations. Some were theorists; some were neuroscientists who were willing to speculate, based upon very limited data and their subjective experience of the Oneness Blessing. And finally, Bhagavan and the dasas at the Oneness University shared with me their vision of what is occurring within the brain.

The point on which every one of these people agreed was that the human brain is one of the most mysterious arenas of investigation for modern science. Countless books and studies have been written in the last several decades, and they seem to agree conclusively about only one thing: there is much that we still do not know about the brain and the relationship between brain activity and our subjective experience. Therefore, in speculating about the effect of the Oneness Blessing on the brain, we can see it not as a work in progress, but as a vision of possibility.

At the time of this writing, no controlled research has been conducted in any scientific institution on the effect of the Oneness Blessing; there are no published pilot studies, although several reputable research facilities are now expressing interest. The first courses to prepare Blessing givers only started in 2004, and of course to get real scientific research done requires advance planning, considerable funding, and, most important, scientists who are interested in investigating the phenomenon more deeply.

What we have instead is a wealth of what a scientist would call "anecdotal reports," some of which use non-conventional methods, that suggest that the Oneness Blessing brings about changes in brain activity, and that speculate about what these changes might mean. One scientist described this as no more than "brain gossip." There has been enough of this gossip, from enough different sources and disciplines, to make this an interesting conversation, albeit an inconclusive one. Most of the people who collected readings claimed that the effect of the Oneness Blessing on the brain was immediate: changes were registered on the equipment being used within thirty seconds, and those taking the measurements felt they could not be explained by the normal fluctuations of brain activity. Furthermore, it was also suggested that these changes are cumulative. In other words, after receiving the Blessing, the brain does not fully return to its baseline state, but retains some of the effects of the Blessing, and further Oneness Blessings would intensify this process.

BRAIN GOSSIP

For example, Dr. Eric Hoffman is a clinical psychologist in Copenhagen, Denmark, who has been using simple EEG readings (or electroencephalograms, a big favorite at spelling bee contests) with his patients for many years, as a form of biofeedback. He teaches people to relax, to focus, or to meditate, and they can see the results immediately as changes in colors on a screen.

Dr. Hoffman told me that EEG readings date back to the early decades of the twentieth century. Small metal electrodes are placed on the scalp at specific locations, and measure the electromagnetic impulses from the brain in microvolts. Results used to be printed on paper measuring two feet across, but are now displayed on computer screens. Readings compare the differential between pairs of electrodes, as well as between a specific electrode and a fixed reference point. With EEG measurements, great significance is given to the frequency of the resulting traces, which are labeled in different ranges as delta, theta, alpha, beta, and gamma. Dr. Hoffman showed me dozens of pictures, created by his software, showing pictures of the brain from above. The software creates different colors to indicate the different frequencies measured at different points on the scalp. He tells me that the changes he sees on these pictures as a result of the Oneness Blessing are of quite a different nature and degree compared with what he has been able to measure using the EEG as a biofeedback device to help people to relax or to teach them to meditate. He tells me he has been unable to reproduce the same results through asking people to self-induce a subjective state.

Henner Ritter, a psychologist in Stuttgart, Germany, took the twenty-one-day Oneness Process in 2005. His colleague and neighbor is Dr. Günter Haffelder, the director of a private research institute with a focus on learning, learning support, and cerebral damage. Dr. Haffelder has developed a form of high-density EEG using a spectral-analysis graphic display to gain a deeper insight in functional and dynamic processes of the brain. Because of the increased number of electrodes and the kind of software he has developed, he is able to re-create three-dimensional images of the brain, and to gain much more information than from simple EEG. He took readings on Ritter both before and after his twenty-one-day course, and saw enough of a change that he also saw fertile ground for further study.

Dr. Susan Schmidt is a retired professor of neuropathology and ophthalmology at Harvard Medical School. Seventy-three years old, she has also been conducting her own tests on the Oneness Blessing, using EEG at a laboratory in Santa Monica that is affiliated with UCLA. Although based on a very small sample group of six or seven people, Dr. Schmidt told me "the parietal-lobe activity was greatly reduced in all the tests, as well as enhanced gamma-wave activity over the temporal frontal cortex."

Readings have also been taken on the effects of the Oneness Blessing using unconventional testing equipment not recognized by mainstream science, but which are nevertheless gaining acceptance, particularly among alternative medical practitioners, and particularly in Russia and in Western Europe. The first of these devices, called Karnak, was developed by the neuropsychiatric department at the University of Milan. Without touching or influencing the subject in any way, it is claimed to measure activity within the brain, as well as the relationship between the brain and many vital organs. It operates by sensing electromagnetic energy output, in both quality and quantity, from a distance of two to three feet. The machine will output measurements for different areas of the brain, showing frequency, magnetic flow, and several other parameters. The AMSAT-HC is a similar device, developed for the Russian space program, which measures electromagnetic frequencies by collecting skin-resistance readings from the forehead, hands, and feet. It then provides a detailed, color-coded picture of the body's energetic health state. It is widely used in Russian hospitals, and by acupuncturists and holistic medical practitioners all over the world.

Both of these unconventional devices have been used extensively by Dr. Ralf Franziskowski and Christian Opitz, whose background is in theoretical physics, to take measurements before, during, and after the Oneness Blessing. The results have been cross-checked against each of the devices and against the Blessing receiver's subjective experience, and they have been compared with readings from subjects who had not received the Blessing. Although lacking any kind of acceptance in mainstream science, these readings are the most conclusive to date in suggesting what effects the Oneness Blessing is having on the brain.

The last means of measuring changes in the brain that has been applied to the effect of the Oneness Blessing has no scientific credibility at all, yet it is relevant because its revelations correlate to the observations of the measuring methods already mentioned, as well as to subjects' subjective experiences. You may remember from Chapter Two that some of the children at Jeerash-ram had developed the capacity to receive information from within, and that Bhagavan had told them that this was the *antaryamin,* the indweller. This kind of direct revelation has continued to grow ever since. There are Oneness Blessing trained surgeons (in India) who suddenly know the right place to operate, quite contrary to any external symptoms, because of an inner knowing.

There is a small group of dasas in India who have the ability to look into the brain and to measure its activity. Bhagavan explains exactly how this occurs:

Since ancient times, in India we have used what is called the antary-amin. A good astrologer not only uses the horoscope; he also consults the antaryamin, which tells him this is how the future is going to be. Similarly, when an Ayurvedic doctor diagnoses the patient, the antaryamin will tell him, "This is the ailment; this is the medicine." Here, we have dasas who have this antaryamin for making measurements of the brain. So they go inside and ask, "What is this person's frontal lobe, this person's parietal lobe?" They get the readings. They can also see into the internal organs: they can see how your heart is functioning, how your brain is functioning. We see dramatic changes occurring in the brain. In certain areas of the brain, activity is getting reduced, and certain other parts of the brain are becoming more active. We have found a way by which we can see whether the activity is going down or the activity is going up. From this, we have come to the conclusion that there seems to be some kind of mutation that is occurring in the brain, the very brain cells, which gives rise to different states of consciousness. It looks as though the whole brain, as well as many of the body's organs, are involved, but for practical reasons we focus more on the frontal lobes and the parietal lobes.

I also spoke to a number of scientists who were conventionally trained in neuroscience. There are now several who have trained to give the Oneness Blessing. Some have taken readings of the effect of the Oneness Blessing, using different methods, but all of them were very reluctant to talk about it, and would do so only under conditions of strict anonymity, from an undisclosed location. I started to wonder if I was trying to investigate what is happening inside the brain or inside another White House scandal. "We scientists are a very conservative breed," one of them told me, anonymously. "It takes literally decades to establish a platform of credibility and respect, and that can be destroyed overnight by making claims for anything that has not been proven.

People think that because it has been written somewhere and they have read it, or because it has been casually speculated about, it must therefore be true and has the weight of experimental science behind it. That is the problem. That is why we do not speculate."

In order for anything to be established in science, it needs to pass through certain accepted criteria. Dr. Schmidt explained that, for any research to be valid and respected among conventional scientists, it must conform to at least these five standards: the research is performed under controlled conditions; it is replicable by other scientists in other locations using other subjects; that it is performed using double-blind protocol; that it is peer-reviewed by other scientists; and that the results are published in scientifically accepted journals.

"Nevertheless," Dr. Schmidt continued, "everyone does it; everyone follows their vision anyway. Einstein called it 'the use of imagination.' He followed his intuition. Of course, it can bias the results when you are expecting something, looking for something. But we cannot avoid the fact that everyone speculates." Dr. Schmidt told me she is now convinced that the Oneness Blessing is having a powerful impact on the brain. Based on her preliminary readings and those of others, she has plenty of ideas of what may be going on, and being retired, she was willing to go on record. "It will be interesting in the next years," she said, "to find out how much of this speculation is validated in the laboratory."

SPECULATIONS ABOUT CHANGES IN THE BRAIN

With the distinction clearly made between disciplined research and casual speculation, the brain gossip about what effect the Oneness Blessing might be having upon the brain falls into five major categories. Not everyone I spoke with talked of all five of these possible changes, but it took several people agreeing on each one to include them here.

1. A Shift from the Reptilian Brain

Although we often refer to "the brain" as a single, solid unit, many who speculate about the brain feel this assumption is not really true. Dr. Paul D. MacLean, a prominent brain researcher, has developed a model of brain structure that he calls the "triune brain." Humans have not one brain but three. MacLean says that the human brain "amounts to three interconnected biological computers," with each biocomputer having "its own special intelligence, its own subjectivity, its own sense of time and space, its own memory, motor, and other functions."

MacLean states that each of the three brains corresponds to a major evolutionary development. The reptilian brain is the most primitive of the three, and constitutes the brain stem. It governs fight-or-flight responses, and is responsible for a lot of basic physiological functions. The mammalian brain, made of the limbic system, is the social brain—it is how we navigate our relationships and our place in society. The mammalian brain is problem-oriented; one could say it lives in a continuous soap opera. The neocortex is the higher brain. It comprises a great deal of what sets man apart from other mammals, as well as higher functions that we are just growing into. As we will discover, it has many different lobes, like stalks of a cauliflower, which are associated with different kinds of activity. MacLean suggests that when a psychiatrist asks his patient to lie down on the couch, he is asking him (the neocortex) to stretch alongside a horse (the mammalian brain) and a crocodile (the reptilian brain).

One line of speculation about the effect of the Oneness Blessing on the brain is that it causes a shift of energy from the brain stem (the reptilian brain) to the neocortex. This was the view expressed more by those using less conventional equipment. They suggest that we are still highly influenced by our reptilian brain, which plays a major role in our aggressive behavior, territoriality, and ritual and social hierarchies. As one neurologist put it, "It can seem like we are living in the twenty-first century with thirty-million-year-old hardware."

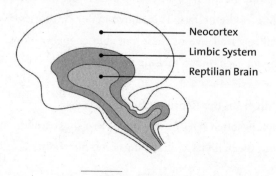

Neocortex
Limbic System
Reptilian Brain

Dr. Hans Selye, who coined the word "stress" to describe a certain mechanism in the human body, suggested in the 1950s that the reptilian brain in humans constantly operates in the state that, for other species, correlates to an actual threat to life. Dr. T.D.A. Lingo showed that if you activate this part of the brain in a cat to the degree of stress that naturally occurs in humans, the cat will run in terror from a mouse.

"The reptilian brain in humans is largely involved in making choices and decisions for which it is ill-equipped," suggested one scientist. "Reptiles do not play; they do not express joy; they have no emotional bonding. They are concerned only with survival. When the reptilian brain is more dominant, we are concerned primarily with survival, too. What feels real to us is determined by neurological intensity. For the brain, facts don't matter so much. When a certain experience comes with enough intense neurological firings, it feels totally real to us. When the reptilian brain is less dominant, there is less of a focus on survival, and so more energy is available to be with things as they are."

2. Balance and Calming of the Limbic System

Doctors like Dr. Craig Wagstaff, whom we will meet in the next chapter, say that overactivity in the reptilian brain is exhausting, and leads foremost to an imbalance of transmitters and hormones in the limbic system. The result is that we become emotionally reactive. Wagstaff suggests that while the reptilian brain is purely wired to physical survival, the limbic system has more sophisticated solutions, which include social skills, social activism, and all kinds of desire and craving—including spiritual seeking. When the limbic system becomes more balanced, we experience less craving and discontent of all kinds, and the body readjusts itself to a place of rest and contentment. The effect of the Oneness Blessing is to balance the limbic system in this way, thereby improving physical health. The limbic system governs all the glands in the body, which, in turn, maintain the balance of our bodily functions.

3. Reduction of Activity in the Parietal Lobes

Dr. Susan Schmidt, among many others, explains that although the parietal lobes are actually part of the cerebral cortex, or higher brain, there is a strong

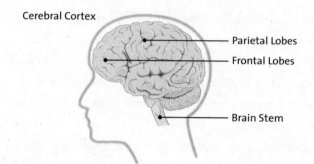

Cerebral Cortex

Parietal Lobes

Frontal Lobes

Brain Stem

relationship between the reptilian brain and the parietal lobes of the neocortex, sometimes also referred to as the Orientation Association Area.

The parietal lobes, particularly the right parietal lobe, give us the capacity, among other things, to negotiate three-dimensional space. You need some activity in the parietal lobes to be able to walk through a door, to put on your clothes, and to know the difference between your body and the outer environment. Dr. Schmidt sees the parietal lobes as a functional extension of the reptilian brain because of their connection with physical boundaries. When survival is at stake, the sense of the body becomes more pronounced, and as reptilian-brain response patterns decrease, automatically there will be a decrease in parietal-lobe overactivity.

According to Bhagavan, the parietal lobes operate at about three times the activity needed to perform their healthy functions. As a result, in addition to being able to negotiate space, the parietal lobes create a strong sense of separation: of a me and a not-me. In this sense, Bhagavan suggests that overactive parietal lobes are the biological seat of the ego: their overactivity creates the illusion of a deficient separate self that constantly needs to do something to solve a problem. Bhagavan explains that when most people arrive at the Oneness Univerity, the dasas get intuitive readings of between 56 and 60. (This scale, by the way, is unique to the dasas and Bhagavan; it bears no relation to EEG readings in microvolts.) They try to bring the readings down to below 30 on the left and 25 on the right. Once the readings come below these levels, they claim that the sense of separation naturally dissolves.

4. Increase of Activity in the Frontal Lobes, Particularly the Left Frontal

In contrast to the parietal lobes, suggested by some to be chronically overactive in modern people, the frontal lobes are said to not receive enough energy. It has been suggested that we use less than five percent of the capacity of our frontal lobes. Hence, the understanding of their healthy functioning is somewhat fuzzy. Textbooks on the brain describe the frontal lobes as the seat of focus, reason, logic, and other "higher functions." I asked one very reputable scientist what these other higher functions were. He confided in me that no one really knows.

Among the suggested changes that happen immediately through the Oneness Blessing, then, is a huge increase in frontal-lobe activity, particularly in the gamma range. The change reflects a marked dominance of the left frontal lobe, often with ratios higher than 1:1.2. Dr. Hoffman in Copenhagen sometimes found twenty-fold increases, particularly in the gamma range, after less than one minute of receiving the Oneness Blessing. He explained that this is significant for two reasons. First, it is the exact opposite of what he feels is usually happening in the human brain—usually the ratio is the other way, as low as 1:0.8, meaning that the right lobe is dominant. He explains that patients with manic depression who are in the manic phase of their illness will also display increased frontal-lobe activity, but with even higher dominance of the right lobe. Second, he claims that these findings on the frontal-lobe activity of the Oneness Blessing givers and recipients duplicate the findings of Dr. Newberg at the University of Pennsylvania, as well as of Dr. Richard Davison at the University of Wisconsin, both of whom have studied the brains of long-term meditators. They both found increased activity in the frontal lobes, with dominance of the left frontal, which became known as the "jolly lobe" because of its association with causeless feelings of bliss and love in test subjects.

Bhagavan explains what the revelations of the dasas tell us about the significance of increased frontal-lobe activity:

We see in these visions that the left frontal lobe is the one that helps you to experience everything around you. If you are drinking a cup of coffee and the left frontal lobe is sufficiently active, you will truly experience that cup of coffee. What happens normally is the right frontal lobe is more active than the left frontal lobe, and it gives a running commentary: "This is very good coffee, maybe it is not so good, or it is Nescafé, or freshly ground coffee," and suddenly it might jump on to something else, like a baseball match or a cricket match. It never allows you to experience what is going on. A differential of at least 20 (again, using their own scale of measurement) *between the left and right frontal lobes gives you a modicum of capacity to experience reality as it is. Anything, when fully experienced, is pure joy and bliss. Even if somebody were to hurt you physically, if you were to fully experience that, it would also be joy and bliss; it would not be pain. You could experiment next time an ant bites you. You could allow an ant to bite you and you could try to do that experiment. Anything, when experienced fully, is nothing but joy and bliss.*

Once again, the revelations of the dasas in India closely match research on meditation and higher consciousness conducted at universities in the United States and Europe. Dr. Newberg summarizes his findings with long-term meditators by suggesting that when the parietal-lobe activity decreases beyond a certain point and the frontal-lobe activity increases enough, the sense of separateness disappears completely. Subjects feel that they are one with everything and everybody in the universe. He calls this "absolute unitary being."

5. Increased Brain Coherence

The last finding area of speculation that was expressed consistently involves the way that the brain operates as one integrated entity. According to Hoffman, the corpus callosum, a nerve cable that connects the left and right hemispheres, shows increased neurological activity after prolonged exposure to the Oneness Blessing, indicating that more information is exchanged between different centers in the brain. He explains that the average human brain shows a variety of neurobiological activity that appears to be somewhat random, as though each part of the brain is doing its own thing, somewhat disconnected from the other centers. He suggests that longer-term exposure to the Oneness Blessing creates synchrony between these various areas. Different centers may be emitting different frequencies and microvoltages, but they do so in a more synchronized dance.

WHAT IS NORMAL BRAIN FUNCTIONING?

Each of these different streams of speculation about brain changes and the Oneness Blessing would be easy to dismiss if it existed in isolation. The Oneness Blessing stands on its own merits with or without scientific validation: it is justified by the power of so many people's subjective experience. The sheer volume of speculation about the effect in the brain—from scientists, Bhagavan, and others—is what makes it impossible to ignore. At the time of this writing, research projects are being planned in several locations. By the time you read this, the results of early pilot studies may be available on this book's website: awakeningintooneness.org. It will be fascinating to find out which of these speculations are validated by research and which turn out to be no more than gossip.

One of the most compelling reasons that this conversation is so important concerns what we regard as normal human functioning. A conventional brain neurologist in an average large hospital would say that the readings we usually find on a "normal" healthy person are the healthy readings for human beings, and that these unusual states are actually pathological. But more and more pioneers are starting to question this assumption. Perhaps the "normal" readings are not as normal as we think. Perhaps our definition of normality is, in fact, a kind of pathology, and what we are seeing here is a return to health?

Professor Haffelder suggests that one of the factors that encourages this inquiry is the notion of "neurological efficiency parameters," which assess how efficiently your brain processes audio signals or visual signals, or how easy it is to recall information or to make decisions that feel good now as well as later. All these assessments improve when the parietal lobes quiet down, and when the left frontal cortex gets more energy. More is accomplished with less effort and conflict. Dr. Haffelder has been able to accurately measure and calibrate these efficiency parameters with a more sophisticated EEG. Since all the results of the Oneness Blessing—as well as of the research done on prolonged meditation practice—point to improved neurological efficiency, we might feel greater confidence that the feeling of separation—and the feelings of survival, fear, judgment, and hatred—as normal as they may seem, are not, in fact, *natural.* Perhaps there is a natural and healthy state of functioning of the brain and nervous system that we can begin to measure and trust?

In the following chapters, we will explore how this healthier, saner, and more natural state of brain functioning can affect our health, our relationships, and what could be its ultimate potential for the individual life as well as for the planet as a whole.

CHAPTER FIVE

THE ONENESS BLESSING
AND THE BODY

D
r. Craig Wagstaff is a naturopathic physician in Vancouver, Canada. Trained in Western medicine, Chinese acupuncture, homeopathy, and a host of other modalities, Dr. Wagstaff has been in private practice for more than twenty-five years and sees about twenty patients a day. He visited the Oneness University in the fall of 2005 and now gives the Oneness Blessing to all his patients.

Dr. Wagstaff feels that the Blessing causes changes in the distribution of energy within the brain, which affects the hormonal system, regulating all of the body's vital functions. He suggests that as the amount of neurotransmitter activity shifts out of the reptilian brain, as overactivity in the parietal lobes is reduced, and as more energy comes into the frontal lobes, there is an immediate effect on the limbic system. He reports a reduction in both adrenalin and cortisol, widely accepted as our "fight or flight" hormones, and that as those hormones decrease, there is a corresponding increase in the production of oxytocin, sometimes known as the "love and cuddle" hormone. These changes—widely accepted to be the signs of reduced stress—go hand in hand with better immune functioning, improved sleep, and better regenerative ability. He reports that they cause a cascade effect throughout the body, affecting the endocrine system, blood pressure, elimination mechanisms, and blood sugar levels. These changes, reported by Dr. Wagstaff and others, are the first and most prevalent health effects of the Oneness Blessing that we will investigate; they reside in the realm of the explicable. Later in the chapter, we will also investigate the other end of the spectrum: stories of miraculous spontaneous remissions from illness, which, as yet, remain inexplicable.

Dr. Wagstaff points out that eminent researchers, such as Dr. Herbert Bensen at Harvard and Dr. Hans Selye, estimate that a much higher percentage of illnesses than we often imagine are psychosomatic in origin; some say as much as 85 percent. He says that, despite this, mainstream medicine often remains preoccupied with the alleviation of symptoms, offering us pills that make us feel better, while ignoring the roots of the problem. The Oneness Blessing, he says, affects the whole person, and physical symptoms often clear up as a by-product. The willingness to integrate the Oneness Blessing into a medical practice requires a holistic orientation, and most of the practitioners you will hear from in this book practice medicine of that kind. The Blessing allows us to feel more, to be more present with what is. When we can feel old pain and hurt, when we can liberate old trauma from the body, many of our physical conditions clear up on their own. Here is Bhagavan:

Many physical ailments that are psychosomatic in origin get healed by deeksha over time. It depends on the strong intent of the healer and the receptivity of the sick person. Compassion is the key. The more compassion, the more is the healing. Compassion grows, because sooner or later, one discovers that there is nobody there inside. You seem to exist, but there is nobody there. Then compassion is really strong. You feel a oneness with the rest of humanity. Once that happens, you become a great healer.

Dr. Wagstaff is one such great healer. He has an extraordinary gift of intuitive diagnosis. When I interviewed him for this book, my digital voice recorder got full after some time and had to be downloaded to my laptop, which took about five minutes. During that short break, he gave me a complete assessment of my health, down to picking up that my grandmother's brother had died of tuberculosis and that my body carries a cellular memory of TB, which was causing slight problems in my lungs. How on earth did he know that?

He says:

When I give the Oneness Blessing, patients respond better to whatever else I am doing. If I am giving them supplements or a cleanse, doing acupuncture or whatever, if I give the Blessing at the same time, the results are much better. The Blessing accelerates the body's ability to heal itself.

Many patients have an imbalance between the hormones that are responsible for "get up and go" and those that are responsible for shutting down and relaxing, digesting their food, having a good rest. Most of these people are wound a few notches too tight: their adrenal system is affecting their blood pressure, causing anxiety and insomnia. As we give the Blessing, their system has better control, a better ability to switch from alarm mode to a more balanced, relaxed function. An unhealthy person is like an ill-tuned piano. The Oneness Blessing is working on a very high level to get the whole system in tune. The more in tune the body gets, the healthier it becomes.

HYPERTENSION

Since becoming a Oneness Blessing giver, Dr. Wagstaff has continued to work with a great number of patients suffering from high blood pressure, the condition perhaps most widely associated with stress. Most of these patients come to him on medication, and most suffer from anxiety and insomnia. He has noticed significant drops in blood pressure during and immediately after the patient receives the Oneness Blessing, and has observed patients' baseline blood pressure maintaining itself at lower levels between office visits. Initially, he was curious to see if this was simply a placebo effect, so he conducted a simple test in his office:

We did the Oneness Blessing on one group of hypertensive patients, and for another group, we just had them lie flat for ten minutes. For the second group, the blood pressure dropped a little bit, but only about ten points on either end. As soon as they became active, it went back to where it was before. With the Oneness Blessing, it also went back up, but not as far each time. They would get new resting points on the high end, from 180 to 170 or 165 for the whole week. Then the next time, it would reset down a couple of notches. Over time, we have been able to get about 80 percent of our hypertensive patients down into the proper range and off their medications.

He illustrates this general trend with the case study of a seventy-five-year-old German woman who has chronic high blood pressure, is about twenty pounds overweight, has no history of smoking, and has a strong history of hardening of the arteries on her mother's side. We will call her Mrs. S.

She had already been seeing Dr. Wagstaff for several years before he incorporated the Oneness Blessing into his medical practice. Her blood pressure was between 210/100 and 160/90, even with medication. She had taken Vasotech, a variety of hydrochlorothiazides, and most of the other allopathic drugs available. They would work for a few months and then become less effective. Coming from a wealthy family, she had seen specialists in Europe and the United States and had visited the world's best clinics. Dr. Wagstaff noticed two other significant factors in her case, neither of which seemed relevant to Mrs. S. First, she was drinking generous amounts of red wine, sometimes up to one and a half bottles in an evening, to allow her to sleep at night. Second, she had a difficult relationship with her ninety-five-year-old mother. Her mother lived in Europe, and Mrs. S had lived off a trust fund controlled by her mother all her life. They fought a great deal. Dr. Wagstaff had already supplemented the allopathic drugs with a variety of naturopathic interventions: changes in diet, phenolic therapy, an exercise program, and homeopathics. He saw that she was under a high level of physiological and emotional stress, quite out of proportion to her life circumstances. "Her body exaggerated her life circumstances," he explained. They were able to improve her condition but could not get her blood pressure to within the acceptable range.

Mrs. S was one of the first patients to whom Dr. Wagstaff introduced the Oneness Blessing. He did hands-on Blessings, with her permission, on a weekly basis. Within six weeks, her blood pressure dropped ten points on the top end and stabilized there between treatments. After three months, it came down to 140/85. As her condition improved, her office visits became less frequent, down to once or twice a month. Her lower blood pressure continued.

There were two other very significant changes in her case, which are typical of the effect of the Oneness Blessing on one's health. First, she went through a dramatic shift in her relationship with her mother. "She stopped blaming her mother for her life," explains Dr. Wagstaff. "She stopped yelling and screaming at her over the phone and, in fact, now spends much more time with her mother in Europe. I would say that she has learned to accept her mother, to accept responsibility for her life; she has displayed spontaneous forgiveness." The second thing was that after years of insisting that she was not an alcoholic but just drank recreationally, she sought out a counselor, admitted herself to a detox clinic, and stopped drinking completely. From Dr. Wagstaff's perspective, this was how Mrs. S's recovery happened: the Oneness Blessing balanced her brain to allow her to face reality more by bringing more energy to the frontal lobes. As a result, she got real with her relationship with her mother and with her addiction. By dealing with those issues, her level of stress went down, and her condition improved.

Kim Yougsen is the chief executive officer of Suwa Kikaku Ltd. in Japan, a real estate company specializing in leisure facilities. With three hundred employees, he has a sales volume of US$25 billion per year. Like most businesspeople in his position, he works under great stress and had developed a serious heart condition. The Blessing reduced his stress right away. "I am short-tempered by nature," he says. "But recently it doesn't bother me. When I have problems, or things are not going well in my business, I still get stressed and feel negative emotions, but the duration is much shorter than before, and I can see clearly that I am having negative feelings and stress. So I am never disturbed by them like before." Despite the fact that he has discontinued his heart medication, his heart condition has healed since he attended the twenty-one-day Oneness Process.

INFLAMMATION

Dr. Wagstaff sees many patients with multiple sclerosis, allergies, and asthma, all of whom he would characterize as suffering from autoimmune imbalance. Like many doctors, he uses a simple test called erythrocyte sedimentation rate, or sed rate, which measures how quickly, in one hour, red blood cells settle in unclotted blood toward the bottom of a test tube. Elevated readings indicate inflammation, a common element in autoimmune diseases. Inflammation has also been associated with cancer. Dr. Wagstaff says:

> One of the things that makes you inflamed is if your body is too acidic. We try to correct that with diet. We also find that if your nervous system is in alarm mode all the time, living in the reptilian brain, it causes a lot more acid and more inflammation. The more Oneness Blessings we give a patient, the more the sed rate comes down. This correlates with reduced symptomology: they have less pain, less inflammation. They can come in and say, "Yeah, I can move my hand now; I can hold a cup of tea." Inflammation and hyperacidity trigger all sorts of biochemical reactions in the body, and they trigger an amazing number of diseases. You hear about taking aspirin for reducing your chances of bowel cancer. Well, aspirin's an anti-inflammatory. There has been a great deal of work, just in the past couple of years, that shows inflammation as one of the common roots in a lot of diseases. Why one person gets arthritis and another person gets cancer, we don't know. Because the balance of the brain induced by the Blessing seems to reduce the acidity, reducing the simple inflammatory marker, it seems to help with pretty much any condition you come up with. Not all of them, but most of them.

DIABETES

Dr. Wagstaff had another patient whose story illustrates the domino effect of healing that is often initiated when the Oneness Blessing is introduced into a healing regimen. One of his regular patients was married to a very conservative medical doctor, whom we will call Dr. N. The wife received Blessings on a weekly basis, but her husband had no interest at all in any kind of holistic approach. He had Type II diabetes and would not look beyond allopathic medication and insulin for treatment, as that was what the establishment approved. After morning fasting, his readings were in the range of 8 to 12 in the Canadian system, equivalent to 230 in the United States, way above the normal range. He had been diagnosed for about a year and was using steadily increasing medication. His wife eventually dragged him in to see Dr. Wagstaff, who suggested dietary changes, an exercise program, and herbs. But Dr. Wagstaff was surprised to see no changes at all over two months. He proposed the Oneness Blessing but was met with unyielding resistance. Dr. N's wife pressured him, and he finally consented, all the while rolling his eyes at the ceiling and complaining. Two minutes after the first Blessing, he fell asleep and slept for about half an hour. The next week, he did not need to be dragged in. "I've slept the best I have in my whole life," he told Dr. Wagstaff. "I have been an insomniac for as long as I can remember. Can you do that thing again?" Dr. N's blood sugar did not change for six weeks, but he kept coming back because of the alleviation of insomnia. He started looking better and had more energy during the day. At the seventh treatment, he told Dr. Wagstaff, "My blood sugar was so low this morning, I didn't give myself any insulin." His reading was at 3, equivalent to 70 in the United States. It was his first morning without an injection in many months. Since that time, his blood sugar has stabilized within the normal range, and he has reduced his use of metformin from three tablets a day to one.

This case is highly typical of what happens when a doctor introduces the Oneness Blessing into a treatment regime. More often than not, the Blessing will address the underlying cause of the symptoms and will only affect the presenting complaint later, almost as a by-product. In this case, it left Dr. N's diabetes unaffected for six weeks but cured his insomnia right away. It was the good sleep that fixed the blood sugar problem—with sufficient rest, Dr. N's body restored its own balance.

A very similar thing happened to Sada Chen in Taiwan. Leading up to the Taiwanese presidential elections in 2000, she was the campaign manager for the only female candidate. Sada was passionate about bringing women into positions of political power, and she put in fourteen-hour days on the campaign trail, in addition to being a mother. When her candidate did not win, Sada crashed. Her blood sugar levels were extremely high, even with a strict no-sugar diet, medication, and injections. In addition, she was taking Adebung for her hyperactive thyroid. Without the medicine, her heart rate would skyrocket to 142 beats per minute, and she would end up in the emergency room. As with Dr. N, the Oneness Blessing first affected her sleep. Since the election, she had been unable to sleep without a sleeping pill. She attended a twenty-one-day Oneness Process at the Oneness University in India, during and after which the Blessing allowed her to fall asleep right away—naturally, without pills. By the time she returned to her home country, her blood sugar and heart rate had normalized, and she had gone off all her medications.

Sada was consulting with Dr. Tong-Yuan Tai, one of the country's foremost authorities on diabetes and a world-renowned physician at the National Taiwan University Hospital in Taipei. He had no model within his training to explain what had happened to her. "Where did you go? What did you do?" he quizzed her. "What treatment did they do with you?" She tried to explain. Some months later, her doctor attended an international medical conference and presented her case. He was ridiculed; no one at the conference was willing to believe that these changes were possible.

FEELING THE FEELINGS

Dr. Wagstaff had another patient whose symptoms were alleviated by the Oneness Blessing through an indirect route. Mrs. R is a forty-three-year-old woman who came in for intestinal cystitis, an autoimmune disease of the bladder that is often mistaken for, and treated as, a bladder infection. In truth, the body is attacking the lining of the bladder. The patient is in constant pain, and not much can be done. Mrs. R had tried all the conventional treatments with very little effect. Initially, Dr. Wagstaff treated her more for the effects of the antibiotics and steroids than for the disease itself, clearing her of fungus and supporting her immune system. But these treatments had no effect on the pain itself. Mrs. R had tried yoga and meditation, and requested that Dr. Wagstaff give her the Oneness Blessing. After two days, the pain went away for the first time in fifteen years. The relief lasted for just a day, and then the pain returned. They continued with Blessings, as well as with her other treatments, once a week. Each time, the alleviation of symptoms lasted for a longer time. After about a month, she started to have very intense dreams of sexual abuse. At first, they were symbolic and required interpretation, but they became more and more explicit. She had no previous memory of abuse. Finally, the dreams turned into very clear images, even during her waking hours, to the point that she was able to recognize what had happened in her childhood and with whom. By speaking to family members, she was able to verify that these memories were, in fact, accurate. By this point, she was entirely pain-free and symptom-free. Because of her inflammation through the whole pelvic area, she had been unable to have sex with her husband for several years. Once the pain, as well as the subconscious trauma, was cleared, she and her husband began to enjoy a regular sex life again.

Mrs. R had not come to Dr. Wagstaff to clear memories of sexual abuse. She was not even aware she had experienced such trauma. Dr. Wagstaff suggests that the increased neural activity in the frontal lobes, as well as a relaxing of the reptilian brain and parietal lobes, allowed her to integrate feelings and memories that she had previously been unwilling to feel. Her physical symptoms dissolved as a by-product.

MIND OVER BODY

Dr. Elena Upton, a homeopathic doctor in Santa Monica, California, lists many Hollywood stars as her clients. She has chosen to focus exclusively on homeopathy because she sees it as the modality that is least symptom-oriented: homeopathy sees everything that is happening in the body, the mind, and the emotions as manifestations of a much deeper energetic imbalance. She works with a diagnostic technology called the Nutri-Energetics System, which she says reads the energetic field. As she describes it, it is "acupuncture in a computer program, and the remedies are like acupuncture in a bottle. I can find energetically where the blocks are. It's extremely accurate. People will come in with blood tests or will tell me what their symptoms are, and I'll run the program, and it will be right there on the screen, showing me what their issues are." Most of her clients are skeptical when they come for their first visit. However, once they see the way the machine can accurately read their medical history and symptoms—without their providing additional information—they are convinced.

Dr. Upton feels that symptoms manifest in the mind before they reach the body. She claims that her patients do not "catch" diseases like cancer, MS, lupus, or chemical sensitivity. She feels that a change happens in consciousness, which then makes the disease consistent with a perceptual bias of themselves and the world. She says:

> I never work with the disease; I work with the person. I look at the situation in a different way than a medical doctor; I look at what's going on in their minds. My observation so far has been that the Oneness Blessing helps my patients open their minds. Illnesses begin in the mind; the Blessing gets all that chatter out of the way; it helps them step out of that. It slows down the mind, so that now they're more in control, instead of their minds running them.

Bhagavan speaks of the effect of the Oneness Blessing on the body in the same way:

> We see dramatic improvement in health because all the ailments that were being caused by negative thoughts, by traumas, disappear in due course. For many people, not only do they go out of the mind, but a transformation also occurs within the mind. They are the ones who become healed. We believe that thought has created this body and the environment. If we can bring about a change in a thought structure, it is accompanied by physical changes. Deeksha has the power to restructure your thoughts. Once that happens, physically things could change very dramatically within moments. When I say a transformation of thought, I mean a change in consciousness; you can do wonders with it. You can materialize things; you can make them disappear. You can do anything you like because you are actually God, and you can create. People do not realize the power that they hold within themselves. Once you realize this, then it becomes child's play.

Dr. Upton has had extraordinary results with her patients in a short time. Mrs. B, for example, came to Dr. Upton with multiple chemical sensitivities that made her a prisoner within her own home. Dr. Upton's office has been customized for chemically sensitive patients, providing Mrs. B with the only place where she could comfortably visit. If someone walked nearby wearing perfume, however, or if a smell of cooking wafted up from a nearby restaurant, she had to leave the office.

Mrs. B earned her doctorate at twenty-three and, soon after, felt that she had done it all. She got married and had two children, but the world seemed to be of increasingly less interest to her. So, Dr. Upton believes, she shut it all out.

There was nothing wrong with Mrs. B physically. She had been through every kind of hospital test available: blood tests, CAT scans, urine and stool tests for parasites. Everything showed up as normal. Her doctors dismissed her and wanted to send her to a psychiatrist for psychotropic drugs. Even Dr. Upton's diagnostic machine could find no cause for the sensitivity. So Dr. Upton focused more on the thoughts running through Mrs. B's mind. For Dr. Upton, the proof that Mrs. B's condition was created more in her mind than in her body came one day when Mrs. B visited the office just after her father had died. She was upset and angry because he lived in another part of the country, and she had not been able to get on a plane to see him when he was in the hospital, and she could not go for the funeral. She was very isolated at home. Her husband and children were out in the day, and she needed to vent. Someone wearing strong perfume came into the office during her visit. Even Dr. Upton reacted to it, but Mrs. B didn't even notice it. She was so intent on needing to talk about her father.

Dr. Upton found several remedies for Mrs. B, but her reaction to each was so severe that she immediately had to stop taking it. They reached an impasse, and Dr. Upton referred her to Lindsay Wagner to receive the Oneness Blessing. The first result, after three weeks, was that Mrs. B became interested in trying new remedies. She wanted to speed up the healing, and became thirsty for things that might help. Her mind had changed. She says that when she receives Blessings, she can actually feel the changes happening within her brain. She now describes herself as not having as much anxiety and mental stress.

She is aware of having been plagued by an overactive mind, which, in turn, created many fears. When her son recently fell ill while away at camp, instead of her usual panic, she was calm and undisturbed. She reports that after the Blessing, her mind becomes quiet, she calms down, and her chemical sensitivities lessen. Although her symptoms are not completely alleviated at the time of this writing, she is generally less reactive to smells and other awkward situations that had set her off in the past.

For many of her patients, Dr. Upton sees their symptoms as indirect ways to fulfill another deeper need. In neurolinguistic programming, this is known as secondary gain. A seemingly unpleasant situation like an illness, which no one would consciously choose, has a hidden benefit that is preferable in the subconscious to some other outcome. In Mrs. B's case, a deep subconscious decision was made in her early twenties to shut out the world, which she perceived as threatening. To the reptilian brain that made the decision, chemical sensitivity seemed a small price to pay for a sense of safety. As the energy moved up into the higher brain, that decision was rescinded, and her symptoms began to recede.

Dr. Upton and other practitioners do not usually suggest that the Oneness Blessing can cure disease directly. Rather, they suggest that Blessings change the balance of energy in the brain, allowing decisions that were made in the lower brain to be re-created in the higher brain; secondary gain based in survival fear is released, and the subconscious motive for disease dissolves.

DEEKSHA AND AYURVEDA

Dr. Sunil Joshi is one of the foremost authorities in the world on Ayurveda, the ancient Indian system of healing. Today, Ayurveda has become a household word, popularized in the Western world by Deepak Chopra and others. Some think of Ayurveda as the ultimate holistic system of medicine: it treats the whole person and considers physical, emotional, mental, and spiritual symptoms as equally valid in both diagnosis and treatment. In Ayurveda, every patient is seen as being made up of three basic *doshas*, or elements: *vata, pitta,* and *kapha.* To put it very simply, pitta is fiery, forceful, driven;

vata is speedy, etheric, mental; and kapha is docile, earthy, slower. For most people, one of these energies is more dominant, which determines their basic constitutional type. In addition, everyone has a tendency, or a weakness, in one of these areas. Dr. Joshi explains further:

Doshas are the factors that distinguish one person from another. If you look inside the body, we are absolutely identical. There is no difference between you and me or anyone else. That is why any surgeon can dare to open your body, because he knows where he's going to find those particular organs in the body. But our bodies do not respond in the same way; they respond differently from one person to another. Everyone responds to surgery, to medicine, to the healing process in a very different way. That thing that makes you different from others is called the intelligence behind the body, the programming of the body—the doshas. It's like a computer. Hardware doesn't make a computer work; it's the software that controls the hardware. If you keep treating the organs, treating the symptoms, and you don't treat the root cause, you're never going to get any better. In fact, you will get worse and worse. That's why it is very important to understand concepts of doshas. Because it gives us access.

In general, the goal of Ayurveda is to restore the balance of the doshas for the person's particular constitution. For example, someone might be born with a natural balance of 60 percent pitta, 20 percent vata, and 20 percent kapha. Such a person would be fairly driven and assertive, with a strong digestion and fairly good immunity to disease. She would still have some etheric, mental energy, as well as the slower, calming energy, but these three elements would exist in a balance unique to her. If such a person were to develop a vata imbalance, say, through excessive travel, late nights, or too much mental activity, she could develop symptoms of vata imbalance, such as nervous disorders or, over time, arthritis or irritable bowel syndrome. An Ayurvedic practitioner would seek to heal that imbalance in the doshas, bringing the person back to her natural constitutional state. Dr. Joshi has found that deeksha (as it is still called in India) balances the doshas in this way, much as his other treatments do. His particular skill is in a modality known as *Panchakarma,* a deep cleansing and restoration of the system that can last from a few days to several weeks. Says Dr. Joshi:

With deeksha, patients are able to transcend and transform their minds and bodies. Panchakarma patients undergo a physical cleansing and an emotional cleansing. Some people can easily start and let go, but they are very few. Most of the time, it's hard for people to let go. With the deeksha, I found they were much more easily able to release and respond to the treatment.

This much we might expect. But Dr. Joshi came to a discovery that, from an Ayurvedic perspective, was much more difficult to explain. When taking the pulse of some of the dasas in India, as well as of other long-term deeksha givers, he discovered that the doshas were not just coming back into balance for that person's particular constitution, but they were also coming closer together into a perfect balance among each other. "This is something I had never experienced before," he says. "It is a very strange experience that I have not yet figured out, quite honestly. It just blew my mind; it blew away all my experience of taking the pulse."

Let us remind ourselves for a moment that Dr. Joshi is widely respected as one of the greatest experts on Ayurvedic pulse diagnosis in the world. He is no beginner.

The doshas are so close to each other that you can't recognize them differently. The pulse of one of the dasas will be almost the same as another: a perfect balance of vata, kapha, and pitta. You have to feel very, very closely to notice any difference, and then sometimes you can feel it. But it looks like a very even pulse.

From an Ayurvedic perspective, this is the physiological equivalent of the dissolving of any sense of separation, any distinguishing signs of an individuated existence. Specifically, Dr. Joshi measured Anandagiri's pulse several years ago, when they were both in New Mexico.

*It was a typical vata-dominant pulse, with vata imbalance. I ex-
plained to him what to do to bring it back into balance. Several years
later, I visited the Oneness University, and Bhagavan asked me to
take Anandagiri's pulse again. It was not the same. Not only was the
imbalance better, it was actually the pulse of a completely different
person, with a completely different constitution. That really blew me
away! These things are not explained in our text in any way. These
things I have never, ever experienced before.*

THE SCIENCE OF THE MIRACULOUS

Earlier in this chapter, we mentioned that the practitioners using the Oneness Blessing are primarily holistic in their orientation. While researching
this book, I searched high and low for conventional medical doctors who
had used the Oneness Blessing. I called all over the world looking for them,
but all I came up with were more and more homeopaths, chiropractors,
and naturopaths.

Dr. Ralf Franziskowski now integrates the Oneness Blessing into his medical practice. "Since I was in India," he told me, "I've watched how things are
happening for my patients. I see that it has less and less to do with what I
learned at university. It requires a different model."

As Dr. Wagstaff suggests, the difference is between a Newtonian way
of looking at the body and a quantum model. Dr. Bruce Lipton has done
extensive research on the mechanics that control cell behavior. His research
points to a radically new way of understanding how our bodies and the
healing process work. Dr. Lipton has been researching and lecturing on cell
biology since 1971, including as a research fellow at Stanford. Dr. Lipton
explains that, for centuries, science has attempted to understand the body
based on the principles of Newtonian physics. This approach views the
body as a mechanism consisting of parts. Pressing button A creates an effect
on B, which will affect C, which affects D. If the body is malfunctioning, it
follows that, as with any machine, one of the parts is broken and needs to
be replaced or repaired.

Dr. Lipton is creating a completely new paradigm for understanding biology. By looking at the body from a quantum perspective rather than a mechanical one, he is the first scientist to provide evidence that consciousness is primary over matter in the functioning of the body. Medicine is riddled with blind spots, he says, and events with no obvious explanation within the current, flawed model. Patients have spontaneous remissions or abruptly get sick for no apparent reason. Conditions can worsen suddenly or disappear overnight. We have all heard of miracle healers and cures, which completely defy modern science and are therefore often discredited as quackery. In a quantum model of the body, what we previously considered to be miraculous has become commonplace. All physical events, including the functioning of the genes, are "overdetermined" (to use Dr. Lipton's coined phrase) by consciousness. A change in consciousness, including one that says whether a condition is curable, how long it will take to heal, how long a life will last, may determine how the cells behave. Dr. Lipton has shown that simply by dissolving belief, we can radically change conditions in the body instantaneously.

In researching this book, I heard dozens of stories from all over the world of miraculous healings, events that completely defy our current medical models. For one woman, her eyesight improved almost instantaneously after a single Oneness Blessing—she even threw away the glasses she had worn to the event. For another, her arthritic pain dissolved instantaneously, and she was able to kneel and sit cross-legged, after having been unable to do so for several years. Virtually every Blessing giver I interviewed had some kind of story to tell of this kind. These stories are often difficult to substantiate or prove medically, but for those who have experienced them, they are impossible to ignore.

Jorgen Ulrik is one such person. A native of Fyn, Denmark, Jorgen was familiar with the feelings and energy that precede cancer forming in the body. His left lung had already been transplanted because of the disease. When he later experienced the same symptoms in his right lung, he went in for a scan. Shadowing on the scan indicated a high probability of cancer in that area, and an exploratory operation was scheduled for the following Thursday. The weekend before the operation, Jorgen attended a Oneness event. When he received the Oneness Blessing, both his Blessing givers felt "commanded" to put their hands on his chest, although neither of them knew anything about the cancer. They both felt a tidal wave of energy pulsing through them for about two minutes. Jorgen says he himself felt blue, red, and yellow crystals exploding inside his chest. He felt his body filling with light and a heaviness leaving his body. When he went in for the operation, the doctors opened his chest and found no trace of cancer. The miraculous result was attributed to an error in reading the scan.

Johan Mansson of Gottenberg, Sweden, had been addicted to drugs since he first smoked hash at age thirteen. He moved on to speed at fifteen and was taking heroin by twenty-four. He has been in and out of jail all his adult life and was homeless for many of those years. When he turned forty, he tried to kill himself with an overdose, but somehow he survived. He was found on the street and taken to a shelter for homeless people and addicts. Yvonne, a woman volunteering at the shelter, asked Johan if he wanted to go to an event one evening, less than two weeks after the overdose. He had nothing to lose. It was an evening with Anette Carlstrom, a popular teacher in Sweden renowned for her powerful Oneness transmissions. Johan was in very bad shape, with cramps all over his body. At the beginning of the evening, he was shaking and sweating all over, still suffering after two weeks without heroin. As soon as he received the Oneness Blessing, however, the cramps and shaking subsided. Each night at the shelter, Johan was required to give a urine sample to monitor any new drug use. Even after two weeks, his body was still full of residue from decades of abuse. He was told it would take at least ten weeks to clear. The night Johan received the Oneness Blessing, the test came up with no trace of drugs. Johan says he slept soundly through the night for the first time in four years. Although the shelter run by the city of Gottenberg will not release any records for addicts, both Yvonne and another volunteer at the clinic confirmed his story for me. He also reports that he has experienced no craving for drugs in the intervening two years.

From a medical perspective, these stories are impossible, but we could fill a whole book with stories just like these. Some may be exaggerations, some may be pure fabrication, but the sheer number of them leads even a skeptic like me to sit up and pay attention.

Like Dr. Lipton, Dr. Wagstaff believes miracles can be the fabric of day-to-day life if we shift our perspective:

There are lots of well-documented cases that show that you can do amazing things by changing someone's energetic balance. When people make peace with themselves and open themselves to the flow of energy, then they can have magical, complete cures. I see the Oneness Blessing as putting them in touch with the design, giving them access to all the information, all the catalyst that they need.

There's a place in Canada, one of the big Catholic churches, where the walls are covered with crutches. The people had to use them to get there, and left them because they didn't need them anymore. We need to look at what we are doing that interferes with the possibility of the miraculous. The more we can get out of the way, whether we're receiving or giving Blessings, the more in line the body will become to that flow of energy.

I asked Bhagavan about the many stories that circulate about miracle healings of these kinds. He responded:

We don't see them as miracles because, from the realm in which we operate, these are very natural things. There are miracles that happen with our knowledge, and some that happen without our knowledge. You might say that we are all the time living in a world of quantum physics. So that's why it's possible for me to appear anywhere on the planet anytime and do these miracles. For me, for Amma, even for some of the dasas, this is the world we actually live in. For us, these are not miracles. There's nothing strange or extraordinary about them because all this is within the realm of human possibility. I think that that is what is going to happen. The whole of humanity will shift in consciousness, and there will be miracles every day in their lives.

CHAPTER SIX

THE ONENESS BLESSING AND RELATIONSHIP

Probably the first and most common arena in which people notice their lives changing after the Oneness Blessing is their personal relationships. Bruhn and Cecile Henriksen got married in Denmark in their early twenties. Bruhn worked at IBM as a communications analyst; Cecile was an account manager at one of Copenhagen's largest advertising agencies. They were both working so hard at making money that they never had enough time to enjoy it.

In his late twenties, Bruhn started to feel a yearning from within. He read many spiritual books and finally got seriously interested in Buddhism. "That started a split between us," Cecile remembers, "because I didn't understand what he was talking about. We no longer had a common language. It's not that I was uninterested; I just couldn't relate to the concepts in the books he was reading. My spiritual life is quite different. I connect with the earth, with the Mother, with nature, through relationship. I felt Bruhn just wanted to get off the planet as fast as possible. It was difficult. I felt wronged somehow." Bruhn agrees that it was like they stood in two different camps.

When his father died, it accelerated Bruhn's inner search, and he and Cecile decided together to take a year off from work to travel in Asia. Even as Cecile learned to relate more to Bruhn's form of spirituality, the loss of intimacy would manifest time and again, creating deep suffering in their relationship. They returned to Denmark with buoyant hopes for a fresh start. Years before, they had fallen in love with an old farmhouse on the remote island of Samsoe. They bought it and relocated. When their daughter, Milla, was born, they initially rediscovered a depth of commitment between them. But the baby also brought new challenges.

Bruhn would go away for several days at a time to work as a consultant, leaving Cecile with the farm and the baby. When he returned home, he was peopled out and craved his solitude and meditation as much as Cecile was craving connection. Time after time, a fight would erupt. She felt disappointed, rejected, and then angry at his self-absorption. He felt invaded, irritated by her needs, and retreated further into his yoga, silence, and ginger tea—always waiting for the next opportunity to escape. During these periods of tension, he felt like an iron gate was closing around his heart.

Their relationship went through periods of relative harmony, but they repeatedly felt dragged into periods of great separation. At these times, a civilized distance grew between them, where terse conversations were exchanged at arm's length. A mountain of unexpressed and unfelt feelings hung over the farmhouse like fog. Then they rarely made eye contact. When they passed each other on the narrow stairs of the old house, Bruhn would step aside just enough so that there was not even a brushing of clothes against each other. Cecile could feel a metallic coldness in her chest and a growing contempt that was very painful for both of them.

Every now and then, the cold war would erupt. Usually she would explode and then throw something or scream. Bruhn had never felt comfortable with outward expressions of rage. He would bottle up his feelings—the muscles in his upper back straining like steel cables under the force of his closure—and not speak to her for days.

As they now recall these unhappy periods, Bruhn and Cecile frequently crack up laughing; they clearly enjoy the memories. "This movie went on repeating itself, on and on and on and on," Cecile remembers. "It was always the same dynamic, just with different headlines." They went into couples' therapy and finally decided to separate. Bruhn planned to move to a spiritual community in New Zealand, while Cecile said she would not leave the farm. All the while, the issue of custody of their daughter and the loss of their dream of a family was tearing them both apart.

Shortly before the separation was due to happen, Cecile knew her usual ways of managing her pain would no longer work. She felt so overwhelmed by pain that she retreated to the tiny attic room that had once served as maid's quarters in the farmhouse and stayed there for a week.

"Bruhn," she said, "I just can't escape what I am feeling. I have to be with it completely. I can't take care of anything but this—and Milla when absolutely necessary." He readily agreed.

She cried and cried and cried for seven days.

"Everything came to the surface. I was seeing everything as it was—all my escape routes were closed down. I saw there was nothing I could do, because whatever I had done had brought me back to the same spot, to the same pain and suffering and separation and self-righteousness. I simply gave up."

It is remarkable how many people come to a point like this just before they find out about the Oneness Blessing.

During the time Cecile was in the attic, Bruhn was mostly alone with Milla. So he took refuge in the lonely man's twenty-first-century companion: the World Wide Web. On the seventh day, he found a site about Amma and Bhagavan and the Oneness University, and printed it out for later reading.

"To this day, I cannot say why I did what I did," says Cecile. "For years he had been printing out spiritual articles, and I had never once taken any interest. But on the seventh day, I walked out of the maid's room, went straight over to the printer, took all the papers he had just printed without looking at them, and took them down to the living room to read them."

"Hey, what are you doing?" Bruhn protested. "I am printing that; those are my . . ." She was already halfway down the stairs.

They both ended up reading it all, and then found more. A softening opened between them. They talked about what they had both read, and decided to take a weekend Oneness course. "From the beginning, I felt my boundaries melting," Bruhn remembers, "like an alien force was being released from my chest." They did more, and then longer, Oneness retreats.

"At first, there was severe resistance," Cecile remembers. "My mind was screaming. I was so fed up. I went out into the woods, and I was crying. When I came back into the teaching hall, my mind felt 'declutched'; it had lost its power. It was quiet and stayed that way for the rest of the seven-day retreat. When I got home to Bruhn, the 'declutchment' was not quite as intense, but it was still there. It allowed a space for healing between us. I was not taking things so personally anymore."

A few weeks later, they agreed that Bruhn would go to the Oneness University to take the course to become a Blessing giver.

After receiving many Oneness Blessings in India, Bruhn, in fact, felt stuck and disappointed. Then one night, all of a sudden, there was a shift. "Next morning, I walked out of the building, and my body was walking all by itself. I was experiencing the mind being totally 'declutched' and presence filling me. When I saw the other people coming out of the buildings, I no longer felt any judgment, no separation, no distance. I was just looking at another me. That had been my greatest suffering: always judging myself and everyone else. Later, I spoke to one of the dasas and explained what I was experiencing.

"'This is just another of those temporary experiences, isn't it?' I asked.

"'Bruhn,' he replied. 'There is no return ticket.'

"He was right. It stayed like that, and it stayed when I got home. The inner judge that made me distant, that made me retreat, that made me close my heart to Cecile, is not there anymore. I had always felt more spiritually advanced than her. I thought her anger was so bad for the environment; it was not spiritual. My spiritual judgment has just disappeared. I no longer feel spiritually superior. We are just equal. It is such a relief. An experience of a deep connection has been lit up; we still have some of the patterns coming up, but they are seen and experienced from a completely different perspective, with much more spaciousness and humor. I can be with her as she is. Even if she becomes angry with me or somebody else, I can fully experience it, and it is fantastic. I feel joy! Sometimes I even feel joy from being angry myself. If she is really hitting the buttons, I watch myself react with a harsh comment and that is totally all right, also. We laugh, and then we stop, and it is gone after five or ten seconds."

Cecile picks up where he left off. "When I was in India, I met the divine within my heart. There is a fullness within me. I no longer have the cravings, the little needs, the strategies that I used to cook up to get something from Bruhn to fulfill me, because I feel full within myself. It is just not possible to take things personally anymore. Now I experience Bruhn as a masterpiece in every aspect. He is like a very strange and interesting exotic animal, and I love him. I love every aspect of him, even those that would have annoyed me and still annoy me sometimes. I used to compare myself, my abilities and talents, with him. There was a constant judging. Now there is no judging; there is no comparing anymore. It is a great relief."

They both feel that the greatest beneficiary of their transformation has been Milla, their daughter. She is thriving in the atmosphere of connection.

"I used to beat myself up constantly for what I did, or how I did or said it. I was constantly judging my performance as a mother, mad at myself if I was angry or not very creative in my response to her. I would carry that with me the whole day or even for several days. I don't carry anything anymore. It's a lighter way of relating. When I am angry, sometimes I express it toward her. Maybe she gets sad, and I comfort her, and the anger is gone. But I don't beat myself up anymore. When I finish being angry, I am joyful. This is a really important example for her—to not "carry over" everything. It's too much heavy baggage; it's just not important. I can see that she is shining. She is very loving and curious. She is curious about everything. It feels very harmonious and easy."

SETTING RIGHT RELATIONSHIP

The story of Bruhn and Cecile is a perfect illustration of how the Oneness Blessing can affect relationships. From the very first courses in 1992, Bhagavan has placed great emphasis on "setting right relationship." The Oneness Blessing works without any effort on the recipient's part; the only thing Bhagavan suggests one can do from one's own side is to attend to one's relationships:

> We have found that the heart plays a very important role. Unless the heart cooperates, we are not able to give higher states of consciousness. In order to make the heart really work with you, relationships have to be set right. And, strangely, we find that the physical heart itself responds very differently after that. And it's as though the heart is sending messages to the brain, and the brain starts functioning differently. If relationships are not in order, the heart just fails to cooperate, and that's where we get stuck.

Rani Kumra, the leader of the Oneness Movement in the United States, puts particular emphasis on setting relationship right in her Oneness intensives. This is due to the powerful impact the Oneness Blessing had on her own marriage.

The Oneness Blessing opens the heart, so you can start accepting people as they are. Otherwise, we are thinking, in an illusory world, that the other person is responsible for our hurt. I have seen it for myself. First you accept yourself as you are. This is how you are; there is no such thing as perfection. When you accept yourself, it is very easy to accept others as they are. Your perception of the other person totally changes. You become more considerate, less controlling, no longer trying to change people as you want them to be. I saw that in my own life. I was thinking the world has to change to fit what I wanted. I was spending energy trying to change other people, which is not possible, which will never happen. The Oneness Blessing changed my perception. I saw that I didn't know how to deal with people—that things could be so simple, and we make them so difficult.

Many psychologists and psychotherapists feel that the flowering of the heart has a neurological basis. They suggest that as long as there is overactivity in the reptilian and limbic brains, deep trauma healing is very difficult—maybe not even possible. These parts of the brain are simply not resourceful. Their instant reflexive reaction to the stirring up of trauma is a strategy to decrease the experience of it. So the full experience of a feeling is not really possible as long as we are running on stress and separation. When we hold a lot of trauma in the nervous system, the relationship is actually happening between those traumatic imprints rather than between any conscious presence, so traumas perpetuate themselves. With more frontal-lobe activity, when trauma is activated, there is a greater resource of awareness. One can be aware that trauma is activated, but one does not have to be imprisoned in it. Because of shifts in the neurological activity of the brain, Bruhn and Cecile had a greater capacity to feel without strategizing, and so to meet on higher ground.

Although they had talked ad infinitum, been to a therapist, and tried everything they could find to save their marriage, none of these things worked, because all were initiated from within the patterns they were trying to heal. When I asked Bhagavan about the various skills we have developed in the West, such as those to create healthier relationship, he commented:

I think all that is very helpful, but the difference is that it is all within the mind. Deeksha gets you out of the mind and allows you to look at things from a new perspective. That's where the real difference is. The kinds of processes that work within the mind are also very helpful and useful. But the deeksha itself works in a very different way. It makes you into a third person and makes you look at your own relationships like a third party. That brings about a dramatic change.

The dramatic change that came over Bruhn and Cecile had less to do with what had happened than with how it was experienced. The old patterns of withdrawal, rejection, and anger still arose, but they were experienced by both in a new way. It was in that mutual shift that they found a new kind of intimacy. Bhagavan speaks about how feelings are transformed through this shift of perspective:

You still get angry. I really do not know how to convey this. This is an anger that has no anger. It is an understanding where there is no understanding. Strangely, all things continue, but they've lost the strength. You can get very angry with your spouse, but the other person does not feel it as anger, and there is really no anger in your anger. You no longer try to understand each other in terms of psychology or philosophy. Everything continues the same, but the core of the anger is missing, and the relationship becomes very beautiful. Couples actually enjoy that anger. Not that they're free of anger, but it has become very enjoyable.

When Bhagavan says this is difficult to put into words, he is not alone. It was difficult to describe for every couple I interviewed whose marriage has been transformed by the Oneness Blessing. The transformation is not primarily of thoughts, words, or actions, but of the space in which these things are now being met. Rather like the magnetic field in which iron filings align themselves, this is an invisible transformation, one that may seem like nothing to the mind that craves change, but is everything to the heart that craves connection.

DIVING INTO PAIN

Every kind of relationship is transformed by the Oneness Blessing, not only romantic or intimate ones. Dr. Eric Hoffman and others speculate that the Blessing shifts the energy from the reptilian brain, which is problem oriented, to the frontal lobes of the neocortex, which give us greater capacity to be sane—to experience things as they are. When I visited Dr. Hoffman in Copenhagen, he showed me countless colored pictures off EEG readings taken before, during, and after the Blessing. I could see big yellow areas opening up in the left frontal lobe when the Blessing was given. Then he showed me a set of readings from a sixty-year-old woman whose daughter had recently died of cancer. She was unable to feel the enormity of her grief and kept it repressed in her body.

The first picture, taken before the Blessing, showed high alpha activity in the back of the brain, as well as some delta. Dr. Hoffman sees this as indicative of the overactive reptilian brain keeping feelings at bay. The second picture showed the readings during the Blessing. I could see the predictable increase in beta and gamma activity in the left frontal lobe. But it was the third picture that was the most revealing. It showed readings for one hour after the Blessing, in which the left frontal activity was still strong, but with increased alpha over the whole brain. I was curious and assumed, from the other readings he had shown me, that in this third picture, the woman must have been in deep peace or meditation. "Oh, no," replied Dr. Hoffman. "Here, she is fully feeling the grief for the loss of her daughter. She broke down sobbing, and the electrodes were still attached to her scalp." What Dr. Hoffman's accidental experiment suggests is that in moments of deep feeling, whether pain or happiness, the brain shows signs indicative of more awakened consciousness.

Since the very first courses in 1992, setting right relationship has been the primary emphasis. Anandagiri, who has been teaching these courses from the start, says:

For a relationship to improve, you must be free of hurt, and you must be free of guilt. Either you have been deeply hurt yourself, or you have hurt someone and you feel bad about it. If you are hurt, the best way to become free of it is to experience the pain completely. And if you have caused pain to someone else, you did so because you could not feel. You did not know what it was to feel that psychological or physical pain. Everything changes when you feel what that person is going through, when you can become that person. When deeksha is given, you can experience your pain completely, and you can feel the pain that the other person is going through. In both cases, your heart flowers—there's the awakening of the heart. You feel more connected. You don't feel separate. There is so much hurt in us, and there is the idea that to be manly, to be strong, one must ignore all the hurts in life and carry on. The more this hurt is avoided, the more you are consumed by it, because it will haunt you all the time. Then we are always preoccupied with thoughts. If you can pay attention to the hurt and pain, listen to it, experience it—it is gone.

The actress Laura Harring experienced exactly this when she attended a twenty-one-day Oneness Process in India:

When I passed through the process of forgiving my mother, I went through an unlayering. I received the Blessing, and right away I saw an incident pass before my eyes of when I felt really deeply hurt. Then I felt the pain in my body, in my belly and chest. It was like a bubble—as I felt it, it released. First there was a picture in my mind, like a photo; then emotion; then it became a body sensation; and then it was gone. To be free, it is not just talking about how much you love them. You have to really forgive them, and this is not about words; it is about feeling. It all concentrated down to one point of pain in my abdomen. I was willing to feel it, and then it went away. I saw a dark cloud lifting from my body, and then there was a lot less thinking after that.

Laura reported to me later that her relationship with her mother has been completely different since that moment of simple feeling.

Time and time again, people receiving the Oneness Blessing report on a simple miracle, that anything felt fully becomes joy, becomes love. As Bhagavan explained, a fight can become a source of joy if it is fully unresisted. He explains that it is actually impossible for this to happen through a decision in the mind. The mind is completely oriented to thinking, with a problem-focused perspective. Some people may think of "brain" and "mind" as almost synonymous, which would be something like confusing the word "stomach" with "nausea." The way that the Oneness Blessing affects the brain brings a shift *out of the mind* into pure experiencing; it does not primarily bring about changes within the thinking mind itself. Then we realize that the incessant activity of thought we call "mind" is actually an aberration of brain activity. The healthy brain does not create endless thinking but instead brings the capacity to experience life in an ecstatic way.

Over the years, both Amma and Bhagavan have met with countless married couples. He comments:

We do not aim to affect changes in behavior but only changes in the way you experience things. We all carry a lot of stories in the mind that manipulate and control relationship. They have to be experienced, and then they lose their charge and no longer interfere with you. Without that hold, relationship naturally falls into order. The person looks very different. I've had so many people complain to me, saying they want to divorce their wives. They say, "I really don't like her. I don't like her face. I don't like her complexion. I don't like her teeth." Once they have listened to the story of the mind and they have received deeksha, the same person falls in love with his wife and the relationship is set right. This happens almost every day.

When we "declutch" from the stories in the mind, forgiveness does not require any commitment or decision; it just happens. Suddenly, what seemed to be important and worth resenting no longer seems important, and nothing remains to forgive.

MOTHER AND FATHER

There are two relationships that are particularly emphasized in Oneness courses and the Oneness Process: the ones we have with our mother and father. Bhagavan explains that these two primary relationships are the foundation of every other relationship we have later in life:

> *If someone complains to me about a problem with the boss or spouse or a friend, I ignore all these things and go straight for the mother and father. We just work on these two with the deeksha, and everything is over.*

Bhagavan explains that each relationship affects us in a different way. An incomplete relationship with one's father creates financial woes, difficulties with the material world. An unhealed relationship with one's mother causes unnecessary obstacles and sabotage, the breakdown of relationship. As we will see in a later chapter on business, at the Oneness University the primary strategy to help companies become more successful is to ask the CEO to examine his feelings for his parents.

Anandagiri has helped tens of thousands of people to free up parental relationships in this way:

> *Karmically, the relationship is only complete when you feel love and gratitude for both of them. Otherwise, you are in debt. When you feel gratitude, you are free—you can move on. You might be separated from your parents, but still you carry them all the time. We cannot ask people to feel grateful; that is not going to happen. If it were that easy, our world would have been transformed long ago. The only way*

to come to gratitude is to feel the hurt completely, so you can forgive and be forgiven. Then the relationship is set right, and you are unburdened. Your whole life changes.

In addition to her TV role as Lady Diana, actress Catherine Oxenberg comes from royal blood. Her mother is Princess Elizabeth of Yugoslavia. During her Oneness Process in India, Catherine went through a profound shift within herself in relationship to both her parents. She felt the sadness she had carried her whole life from trying to win her father's approval, but nothing dramatically shifted. It was only when she got home that she realized something had changed.

Catherine's father is eighty-six now and suffers from Alzheimer's disease. Before she started to receive Oneness Blessings, her father would call once a week and yell at Catherine and her daughter at the top of his lungs. He could not control his rage; his disease made him hostile and belligerent. Since she returned, she says, her father has become a completely different man and cannot raise his voice at her at all:

He lives in Florida, but he came out to California to see me. He just could not stop saying loving things. It is a miracle. When we are together now, we simply experience joy. Our family dynamic used to be so hostile that everybody was triggering everybody, and everybody was pissed off with everybody. Each time I interacted with either of my parents, I would become a wounded teenager again, and we would all fall back into these ridiculous roles. Since India, it is completely gone. I have been set free of all that dysfunctional family dynamic that I have lived with my whole life. Through that, all my primary relationships have been totally healed. Real spirituality is not about loving humanity immediately. It is about loving those who are closest to you. And from there, from that strength and that truth, that nucleus, you can radiate out further, into society and then globally. It has to start at home. I'm so eternally grateful for this. We try to talk about it when we give Blessings to people, but it's not until we touch them that they understand.

Then you see the glow on their faces, and they say, "Oh, I get it now." It's something so familiar and so sweet and so precious, and yet it's so easy to overlook because we are usually so stuck in our minds.

This kind of completion with one's parents can occur no matter how great the perceived breach. Many of the people I have interviewed had experienced complete abandonment and estrangement from one of their parents, or even physical or sexual abuse. Although the depth of the pain waiting to be felt might be much greater in those cases, and the hurdle of forgiveness might be set much higher, the power of the Blessing can bring us to gratitude. The healing seems to be not so much concerned with the personal relationship itself, but with the bigger relationship of the masculine and feminine principles universally, of which the relationship to mother and father is just an icon.

This completion can occur whether or not a parent is still living. Nahuel Schajris's mother was a multidimensional woman: a therapist, a schoolteacher, an artist, a dancer, and a filmmaker. When she died of heart disease, Nahuel was in his early twenties. He loved her so much and simply could not feel the pain. While attending a longer course in India, the Oneness Blessing allowed him to fully experience the pain of the loss of his mother:

It was a physical pain. I cried like I'd never cried before. My body was contorting, jumping—it was like losing a part of my body. It was very painful, but at the same time extremely joyful because finally I could experience that pain and express it. I started shouting, "I miss you. I miss you. I wanna see you. I want to see you, Mother." Then I felt her presence. I felt her put her hand in my hand. After forty-five minutes of crying and having all of this, I went to the bathroom because I was all dirty. I was still saying to myself, "I wanna see you. I miss you. I wanna see you." I looked up, and in the mirror, in my face, I saw her face. She smiled back at me, and I heard these words in my head: "You can see me every morning when you see yourself in the mirror. You are part of my body." She was saying that to me and smiling. I was so happy because I totally realized that she's living.

She's living, and she's seeing me, and she sees my brother and sister, and she knows what we are doing, and she's sharing all our happiness and all our pains from where she is right now.

ONENESS BLESSING ON THE COUCH

Because of the extraordinary effect of the Oneness Blessing on completing trauma and healing relationship, psychotherapists all over the world have integrated the Oneness Blessing into their practices. For example, Dr. Ralf Franziskowski, says:

In my private sessions and therapy groups, I feel more and more that there is an atmosphere that has nothing to do with a separate entity called "me." It is this atmosphere that takes my patients deeper, and they come into focus more quickly. There is no sense of a separate "me" doing anything, and it is so freeing when that is not there. They trust so much more; they trust in life.

Lynn Marie Lumiere is a psychotherapist in Oakland, California, specializing in relationship issues. She is also certified in somatic therapy. After she did the Oneness Process in India, she started to use the Oneness Blessing with some of her clients by transferring the energy through intention or by putting her hands on their heads in the course of doing hands-on somatic work.

Sometimes the shift in perspective is sudden and dramatic. One deeply traumatized client who was working on her negative relationship with herself felt unlovable and unworthy. She was constantly feeling victimized by her circumstances and complained bitterly about her life. Lumiere reports that after the woman's first Blessing:

She looked around the room as though seeing things for the first time. She reported seeing beauty in everything and experienced a delight in simply seeing the tree out the window, the color of the flowers in the room, the sounds, and so on. She was just right here in the present moment. She said, "Oh, my God! This opens up a whole new world! I feel so whole and complete just being here. There is so much joy in simply being. I have a knowing inside that everything is just okay, just as it is. And I feel held in a love that is within and all around. It is so beautiful!"

Lumiere reports that the shift in this and several other clients has been stabilized over time.

Another of Lumiere's clients, who was habitually angry, reports that the Blessing has changed her experience of being in the world and relating to others, which had been an area of great trouble for her. She was self-conscious and could not look people in the eyes. After receiving several Blessings, the client reported to Lumiere:

The effect the Blessing energy has on me during therapy sessions has been very noticeable. On some days, questions and problems regarding various issues become less stressful, as I suddenly see the answers very clearly. On other days, after receiving the Blessing energy, I go out into the world and feel like a normal person. What I mean is that I can look people in the eyes and feel okay about myself. In fact, many times I go out and all kinds of nice things happen to me. People smile at me; they come out of the woodwork to help me. I encounter kindness and niceness. I perceive things differently. I feel less threatened and more loving.

DIVINE RELATIONSHIP

For a number of people, the Oneness Blessing has not only cleared up dysfunctional patterns in relationship, but it has also catapulted them into a completely new way of relating altogether. In Chapter One, I mentioned that one of the things that most impressed me when I first visited the Oneness University was the relationship between the dasas. There have been many

Eastern teachers and teachings that have affected the West in the past few decades. The great majority have become mired in politics, as competition to get to the top and to be closer to the leader eclipses the original mission. Although the Oneness movement has had its share of political fallout among its Western representatives, the relationship between the 170 dasas themselves is extraordinary and has been a breath of fresh air, an inspiration, for many Western veterans of organized spirituality. I myself was highly skeptical after being introduced to the Oneness University, and presumed that there would be the same political intrigue and backbiting that I had encountered elsewhere. I have really looked. In the research for this book, I spent many days with Anandagiri and Samadarshini, and watched them interact with the other dasas. During the more than seven weeks I spent at the university, I cannot recall a single instance of impatience, stress, or conflict among the dasas. Find me another spiritual organization where this is true. Many of the dasas are sleeping fewer than two hours a night and dealing with hundreds of Western visitors a day—not to mention juggling phone calls and e-mails. I asked Anandagiri how they manage, and he replied:

> We have never thought about it. I think that just being with Amma and Bhagavan, we have become like that. We never had this idea that we should be nice to each other or be like a family. It is just like that. And until somebody points out how beautifully we live, we don't even notice it. I do not know how it is in other organizations. Perhaps spiritual ambition and concepts are not there for us because we have experienced so much, all the dasas. We have been given so much that we can't ask for more. We are very simple, very satisfied people.

I also asked Amma and Bhagavan about their experience of their own relationship. Amma responded:

> We are one. We relate to each other as friends. Sometimes Bhagavan makes his decisions and I make my own. In spite of our decisions being different, the ultimate destination both of us reach will always be the

same. We are the mother and the father aspect of the divine. Bhagavan gives people grace as the father. As the mother, I fulfill their desires, answer their needs, take care of health problems, everything. Bhagavan is concerned with the spiritual growth of people and leading people toward liberation. Bhagavan is focused on that, while Amma is immersed in fulfilling people's desires. After my marriage, my husband was always with me. For thirty years, we had never been away from each other. For the sake of dharma, for the past two years, we have been living away from each other. However, even if we are separate physically, as the antaryamin, internally we are one.

Bhagavan spoke of his marriage in a similar way:

We don't have a personal life. We do not discuss personal matters like a normal couple does. Ours is only a public life. We only think about the devotees, the movement, the dasas, and what we should do. It's really that kind of talk. There's nothing personal because there's no personal life. There's no person there inside to have a personal dialogue. It's absent.

He spoke also of his relationships with his mother and his son, Krishna:

My own mother died on my lap. There was suffering, but it was not personal. I felt suffering because I could see she did not want to go. So that did affect me, but not as a person—not that it was "my" mother who was passing away. It didn't affect me that way. Of course, I helped her out, and then she finally passed away very joyfully. It's a question of shifting your stance from being involved to being a witness. Because it was not my mother, that kind of stance was not there. I saw a beautiful being, who has helped me so much, passing away. And I know where she's going. So, in a sense, I'm happy. But I saw the others in tremendous grief. That was affecting me. It is the same thing with my son, Krishna. I know he is my son, yet my relationship is like that of a third person. I relate to him like I would relate to any dasa. There's no difference at all. In actual relationship, there's no difference. But I do know he's my son. Sometimes he demands, "You have to be a father to me." Sometimes I put on an act for him, and he knows that I am putting on an act. I make some inquiries like a father would do. And then he feels satisfied.

I also asked them both how they relate to the rest of the world, to the nearly seven billion human beings and countless sentient beings on this earth. Amma responded:

All of humanity is one being. All humans are actually one person. You should not think that "what is going on in me is something different and unique from others," that "my thoughts are different from the rest." It is humanity's suffering that is flowing through us. You need an inner spiritual experience to know and feel this suffering completely. That is when the state of love would take root in you. You can know this only through experience. There is no other way. Therefore, what is going on in the other and what is going on in you is not different. All . . . all is one. Only when you have this experience is the state of compassion possible.

CHAPTER SEVEN

THE ONENESS BLESSING
AND YOUTH

Growing up in today's world can be a bewildering experience. When kids look at their world, they see global warming, depletion of oil, apparently civilized countries involved in torture, vast and incomprehensible economic disparity, a feeding frenzy of commercialism. It is a madhouse. Many young people feel powerless. As the stability of the family has eroded in Western society, kids can feel lost and insecure, doubting whether they are loved. Particularly in America, commercialism has taken over every area of life: at school, in sports, in art. Many kids feel used as consumers. It is easy to lose track of any core values or direction. When I conducted interviews with college students for my previous book, *The Translucent Revolution,* the words I heard most often were "powerless," "overwhelmed," and "lost."

The Oneness University in India has put a strong emphasis on helping the younger generation during the past years—mostly with Indian youth, although it is now starting to spill over to the rest of the world. Since 2004, more than 52,000 kids from all over India have participated in a six-day youth program, with extraordinary results. Bhagavan explains his vision for these courses:

We want youth to become less self-centered, to be loving and joyful—not the kind of joy and love you get with comfort, but unconditional love and unconditional joy. We want to create very happy people, because with happy people, it will be a happy world. For them to be happy, they should be free of the sense of a separate self. We help them to fully flower into human beings. The full flowering of the human being is nothing but the flowering of the heart. Society must be so structured that the heart of the child does not wither away.

It is a simple transformation for the heart to flower, and then there will be heaven on earth. We are creating enlightened youth who are world citizens—who care for those around them, who are not concerned only with nationalism or one particular religion. We need a world where there are no national boundaries, where there are no racial boundaries, religious boundaries—no boundaries of any sort. I think these young people will emerge like that.

Samadarshini has been designing and leading these courses since their inception. She explains that the basic six-day course is for people from fifteen to thirty—for those who are still studying or who are just staring a career—and each includes 120 to 150 participants. Most come because they have been so impressed with the results in friends or colleagues, while others are sent by their parents. Each of the six days of the youth course explores a different theme so that, at the end of each day, they have a specific insight or shift. If it has not flowered for each of them, the dasas sit with them until a specific outcome is reached. Samadarshini explains:

This land at the Oneness University is very sacred to us because it has been made wet by the tears of gratitude of many a parent. We intend to create successful individuals but with compassionate hearts. If a human being is successful but has no heart, he becomes a danger to society as well as to himself. If a human being is good and kind and loving but continually fails in life, he would sooner or later lose trust in life, become bitter and unhappy. What happens to these young people in six days is phenomenal. Only if one is a part of it could one believe that it is possible. The course consists of a variety of teachings but includes deeksha (as it is still called in India), which makes every teaching into a personal realization.

Samadarshini explains that although the curriculum of courses at the Oneness University is always changing and evolving, each day of the course, at this time, focuses on one major issue that the participants face in their lives.

Day One: Vision

Samadarshini explains that the first day of the youth course focuses on their vision for life:

So many of the youth who come here lack any vision at all. They are just flying around like dry leaves, wherever the wind carries them. On the first day of the course, there is huge resistance. They feel it is boring; they all want to leave. But a life without a vision is like a journey without a destination. It is the vision that we have for our life that gives meaning to our existence. The greater the vision, the greater the human being you become. So we help the youth to find their own vision for life. Each one has their destiny; each has their own reason as to why they are here. We help them realize why they are here. They find a vision for life, and they start to make plans for it. We help them see where their obstructions are; we help them to become thinking individuals.

Day Two: Relationship with Parents

The second day of the youth course is devoted to setting relationship right with their parents: to feel both the pain they themselves have bottled up and the pain they have caused their parents. Samadarshini explains:

By the second day, at least 95 percent of them have changed completely. The second day is a very big hit because they come to terms with themselves; they discover self-acceptance. The next breakthrough comes when their relationship with their parents is healed, because that is the central foundation on which life's edifice is built. They experience the pain their parents have gone through. Before the end of the day, they discover so much love for their parents that all hurts are forgiven. All their pain, all their wounds, are healed, and for the first time, they become sensitive. They realize the pain they have been causing through being self-centered; they realize that they have not been connected to their parents, that they do not know their parents, that they have not felt their parents' desires, fears, and anxieties. They get in touch with their parents, which gets them connected to life, and that makes them very, very secure. They overcome all the resentment and hurt they have stored. After that, all their other relationships fall into place. They often feel very hurt with their teachers, they feel humiliated and insulted, and they get over that, also.

In fact, many of them want to rush out from the course on the second day to go and be with their parents to tell them how much they love them. No matter who their parents are or what abuses they have suffered, no matter what their past, they discover love toward their parents, and later that love begins to manifest as love for their brothers, sisters, and teachers.

Day Three: God and Grace

On the third day, participants are guided to explore the image they have been carrying of God. Samadarshini explains that once the relationship with one's parents has been set right, it will be immediately reflected in one's relationship with the divine:

This is the day where they learn how to pray, how to connect to the divine. Without a connection to the divine, everyone is an orphan. It does not matter what name, what form, we give to this divinity. The students find a connection with their personal God, and their hearts open to the possibility of miracles. Many experience immense healing of the body before the end of the course. Bhagavan speaks of the divine as an "observer-dependent phenomenon." God is like clay, and you are the potter. You can give the divine any shape you want. We ask the youth to observe the perception they've had of God until then. Is God somebody who is very slow in giving blessing? Is God somebody who

tests them to no end before He blesses? Is God somebody who is expect-
ing them to be pure and perfect before He gives grace? What is their
perception of God? We ask them to observe what their image of God
has been and to see how it has affected their life.

As these things get cleared, participants learn how to connect with the divine through the heart. The Christians feel Jesus more, the Muslims connect more deeply with the prophet Muhammad, and the Hindus may feel Krishna or Rama. Some of the participants develop an inner relationship with Amma and Bhagavan, and some just feel the divine as life itself. But all of them speak of a grace, a guidance, and inner communion helping them in their lives, helping them to make decisions and to be secure in moving forward.

Day Four: The Nature of Mind
Samadarshini continues:

Ultimately, everyone has to deal with themselves. Universities and
colleges provide us with skills to survive, but they do not educate us
how to live. We have to deal with ourselves. On day four, participants
learn how to deal with their own minds, with what happened in their
childhood, and with the various personalities that exist in them, with
their unconscious mind and their conscious mind.

Day Five: Intelligence and Creativity
On the fifth day, the students receive a powerful deeksha (as it is still called in India) to rebalance the energy in the brain. They recognize the difference between making decisions from accumulated beliefs and making them from a pure response to the present moment. They learn the art of going into pure silence and allowing decisions to arise from there. They also see the deeply rooted patterns of control and domination, the desire to have things our way, to be right and to make the other wrong, and how this clouds intelligence. Samadarshini comments:

*For many of them, on this day, their inner guide, or connection with cos-
mic intelligence, is established. They discover an inner silence, and they
develop an access to that silence. They get in touch with their higher self,
their indweller, which thereafter begins to guide them through life.*

Day Six: Leadership and Responsibility

Finally, these young people get a sense of being part of a larger whole, recognizing that they cannot be obsessed with themselves alone. They realize that
life becomes meaningful when you contribute to something bigger than your
own immediate needs. They learn how to empower other youth with what
they have learned in their six days. Samadarshini explains:

*When this flowering of responsibility happens early in life, people be-
come a blessing to the world in which they live. They discover that
happiness lies only in helping another. Pleasure is when one helps oneself; happiness is when one is able to help another. They are given a
special deeksha that gives them the power to heal others. They find the
knowledge, the wisdom, through which they can help their friends and
the society in which they live.*

*By the end of these six days, they are complete individuals, indi-
viduals who have total balance between the head and the heart.*

• • •

Having a teen and a preteen myself, I was highly skeptical as to what could
be achieved with a group of adolescents in a few days. This is an age group
famous for its rebelliousness and rolling its eyes to the ceiling. When I shared
my doubts with her, Samadarshini asked me if I would like to meet some of
the participants. After completing the six-day course, many are invited back
for a longer, fourteen-day advanced leadership training, which is free. More
than three thousand young leaders pass through this program each year. By
coincidence, this advanced course of more than 250 graduates was due to
convene a few days later.

And so it was that I found myself sitting on a manicured lawn, facing an army of bright-eyed, brown-skinned laughing buddhas. Cynicism and all, I was inspired and surprised. This group of young people was not fanatic or zealous; they could laugh at themselves and respect differences. For young people, they were extraordinary because they were enthusiastic—not about a movement so much as about life and hope. They were upbeat and confident; they had an "I can do it" presence. For Indian youth, who can be quite modest in their ambitions, these kids were on fire to make something remarkable of their lives and to contribute to the world. The atmosphere reminded me of a motivational seminar more than a spiritual group. It was not just their stories of success and healing that inspired me; it was the light in their eyes, the spontaneous laughter that erupted so easily, and the way they applauded and touched each other like family.

They spent more than three hours sharing their stories with me. Indira's father had left home when she was only two. She had grown up hating not only him but all men, and got into frequent fights with car mechanics, with bus drivers, with her neighbors. She explained:

Through the deeksha, I was able to know what kinds of feelings my father was having when I was little. When I got home, I wanted to tell him I was sorry. When I saw him, I could see he has trouble expressing himself. Then I knew—he and my mother separated for whatever reason, but he still loves me. He told me how bad he felt about not taking care of me, about leaving me and my mom. Now everything has changed; we are friends. I have a very close relationship with my husband now, and no more fights with car mechanics and the neighbors.

Santosh discovered a career in software engineering after the youth course and quickly rose through the ranks. His family was poor and had used what little they had for the children's education. Within a couple of years, Santosh could buy his parents a house.

Many of the students found it much easier to study and pass exams; many overcame their fear of public speaking; many talked of a sense of ease and trusting their inner guidance. And, of course, almost all of them had remarkable stories to tell of a healing in their relationship with their family.

The person who left the strongest impression on me that day was a young woman named Jaya. Born in a rural area, at eleven months she was afflicted with polio. It has left her visibly handicapped: her left leg is turned in almost ninety degrees, and she drags it along as she walks. From as far back as she can remember, she was convinced that both her mother and older sister did not like her. To be afflicted with polio in India is a huge handicap. Jaya told me that her chances of marriage or even getting any kind of job were minimal. "I was really very confused as to what I would do with this life. Would I just die of no use to the family or to society? Would I ever be able to find a job? All those questions were haunting me."

From the first weekend Oneness course that Jaya had attended, before the youth courses even started, everything turned around. Today, Jaya has an extraordinarily relaxed confidence about her. She is married to Venkatesh, a successful young artist and software executive, and they have a young son. She moved up quickly through the ranks of Chennai's thriving computer industry, and in addition to her position as a user interaction designer in her company, she and Venkatesh have founded their own thriving Web design company. Jaya tells in her own words what happened:

Before attending the youth course, I was not a very open person. I would never go to people and talk to them on my own. After the course, I saw that I could handle people. Whatever their problem, I can help them; I will be able to satisfy them. Everybody could see the difference in me. Now, when I have some doubt, I do not mind voicing my opinion in public, in a way that people rarely do. Even in a crowd of a hundred people, I can talk. I do not know how the leadership quality developed, but I can tell you now that I'm a very successful leader. When I came out of the course, I was different. We have so many blocks inside us that we can't raise our voice in public. Even though we have the potential to do it, these blocks inside are stopping us. It's only our perception of ourselves that makes these blocks. On day six, they talk about what it is to be a leader. It is not commanding people but work-ing with people. Leadership is bringing people along with you.

I left that afternoon on the lawn with two burning questions. First, how on earth did you guys pull this off? I have worked with young people in the United States, and my wife has worked as a counselor in Norway with teenag-ers recovering from addiction. Changes at this level usually take months and have a very high recidivism rate. Samadarshini tried to answer this question:

There may be elements of psychology, of philosophy. Those are the things one can describe. But there are other factors that are much more important. First, the guides who are conducting the courses are all in a very elevated state of consciousness. They are people who are com-pletely healed. As they are speaking, they love the people who are in front of them; they love the youth. The second thing is the presence that pervades the whole campus here. And the third thing is the deeksha. That is the integral element. Without the deeksha, none of this could be possible. Every day, each student gets a hands-on deeksha from one or more of the guides. That is why it works.

I asked many of the youth the same question: Why did this work for you? Many of them had attended other motivational courses with little or no result. The answer was always the same. Here is Santosh, a twenty-three-year-old engineer:

There were changes that happened in the brain. I could feel that. Pat-terns that were creating failure and demotivation and demoralization changed to positive forces. It is a change in the neurons, not in concepts or behavior.

Bhagavan concurs:

Ninety percent of the youth who attend change dramatically in six days. The remaining ten percent may have to come for another course. This is happening because we are able to physically transform the brain; it is a neurobiological transformation. That's why we get these dramatic changes: they are permanent, irreversible, and dramatic—you can see that. That is why even the state government has taken notice of this now. They have been sending us the hard-core violent people who indulge in terrorism. These people go back as nonviolent people.

My second big question was, Can these same results be achieved in the West, with Western youth? Samadarshini was honest with me and confessed that she did not know for sure:

We have not tried these courses on the rest of the world yet. But I think it should work, because the principles that go into it are universal. Whether you are American or Indian, your origins are your parents. The way that we experience pain in our consciousness is the same.

I pointed out that the degeneration of the family is much greater in the West, where some kids may have suffered physical abuse or abandonment. In her usual upbeat way, Samadarshini's answer was confident: "If the situation is worse, then the need for healing will be greater, and there will be a stronger calling to the divine. The greater the need, the stronger is the power of the deeksha that flows."

There are plans to have courses in India specifically for Western youth, at very reasonable rates. Perhaps they will be in full swing by the time you read this. But to find out about the potential of deeksha for Western youth, I had to do some detective work.

THE AWAKENING OF WESTERN YOUTH

Alex and Dorian Kingi are among a small but growing number of Western youth who have taken the twenty-one-day Oneness course in India. They went because their mother, Lindsay Wagner, had already been through the

Oneness Process and encouraged them to go. Dorian is twenty-three, lives in Los Angeles, and works, when he can, as a stunt man and an actor.

> *It is hard when you are young and desensitized by movies and television and loud music and fast cars. It is hard to tell what is fantasy and what is reality. Most of us are afraid of anything we are offered now. Is this a temporary fix, or is it going to work? Most people have been offered all kinds of highs by people who want to make money off of you. The world is a scary place just now. We are taught not to feel certain emotions, not to cry or to feel too much bliss. We are trained to look to an external source. When I first went for a Oneness Blessing, I was very skeptical; I am afraid of organized religion and all the political aspects. I really didn't feel much at the time. I felt kinda relaxed, but nothing extraordinary.*

The next morning, his mother called him to see how it had gone. She was used to the fact that he sleeps late and then wakes up grumpy for a while. He was not usually fit company till about noon. She really wanted to call, and waited till ten, knowing he would still be asleep.

"Hi!" he answered.

"Are you awake?" she asked.

"Yeah," he replied. "The birds are singing, the sun is shining, and it's a beautiful day!"

"Wait a minute, is this 818-935-67 . . . ? Who am I talking to?"

Dorian received the Blessing a few more times over the following months, and his energy continued to rise. By summer, he and his younger brother went to India to become Oneness Blessing givers. Dorian describes several shifts in his life since then. First, he says that he used to have a hard time finding work as an actor. He was frustrated and would work only a few days at a time every couple of months. When his plane touched down after the twenty-one-day course, "there was a message asking me if I wanted to start prepping for a show with Kevin Costner and Ashton Kutcher. It was six weeks of work. I was just like, 'No way.'" He reports that he has been working without a break ever since.

Second, he speaks of a much greater capacity to be himself:

Everybody says you have to have a nice car, really big rims and tires, and a loud stereo system to be the cool guy. You put on a front to show people that this is who you are, but really you are pretending to be somebody else—because, otherwise, you are not cool or accepted. The sad thing is, when you try to be something you are not, you fail even more. That has really shifted for me, because I now feel more content with being myself and being alone. I don't need to have other people around me to complete me.

A lot people are afraid to be by themselves. Kids are afraid to be by themselves because then they're not cool. "Hey, what are you doing?" and then you're just, "Oh, I'm just hanging out at home." "Oh, you're a loser, man. Why don't you come hang out with us and party?" I hang out when I choose to, but I can also go and be by myself.

The third thing he noticed is the quality of leadership:

What I have experienced and now know is that by being myself and being happy, I will be the basis and the template for others to see and experience happiness. We have a youth meeting at my house now, where there are usually about fifteen people or so. We have a little dinner and then a little youth group, and I give my friends the Blessing. If I am happy, others also become happy. It has to start somewhere.

Alex is four years younger than his brother and has similar stories to tell. He says he was always more comfortable to be with his brother's friends than with his own, as he was around them a lot as a child. He would feel intimidated by people his own age and would quickly make comparisons—who had the better grades and, later, who was making more money.

Now everyone is more like the same. I do not pay as much attention to people's ages. If someone my own age is doing well, I am impressed. I feel inspired by what they have done instead of feeling pushed down by it.

The biggest change was with his father, who left the family when Alex was still quite young. Alex had felt fear and apprehension whenever he saw his father, concerned about how they would get along. He brought all this to the twenty-one-day course. Right after getting back, Alex went to a family wedding with his father:

I was nervous about what I was going to do and what I was going to say. I just went in as myself, and I let go of all my expectations. There was no attachment. We were able to talk without being afraid to lose one another.

Just as Bhagavan predicted, this resolution, forgiveness, and shift into gratitude with his father had an immediate effect on Alex's material and business life. He had an idea, very playfully, to start an organic cotton clothing line with his brother:

It wasn't something I had to make myself do; it was something I wanted to do. We talked about it. Organic cotton clothes are often expensive, and we wanted to make them affordable for people our age. Then a couple of days later, we met a woman who is an organic cotton distributor from India. They had a way to ship it instead of flying it in, so that makes it much cheaper.

Things fell into place for Alex without much effort at all.

There are hundreds of parents who, after they come home from a course, give the Oneness Blessing to their kids. Catherine Oxenberg has a teenage daughter who had been quite dyslexic, averaging C's and failing at math. After three Blessings, Catherine reports her daughter was getting A's. She has given Blessings to many of her daughter's friends, too:

Our fourteen-year-old invites her friends over and asks us to give them the Oneness Blessing. I find it works much faster with the youth than with us older people. When we give the Blessing for the first time to children and their parents, it's the children who immediately connect to the source of the divine. The adults may just say, "It's a pleasant experience. I feel peace and joy." But children immediately say, "I experienced God." Our kids come and ask for it. They say that a family who prays together stays together. I'd say that for a family who gives and receives Blessings together, it creates a harmonic alignment that creates such a beautiful flow in the family. It defies words.

Catherine's husband, Casper Van Dien, feels the same way:

It's a loving thing to be able to do with your children, a very intimate thing. Catherine and I give the Blessing together. I put my hands on people's heads, and she puts her hands on their hearts at the same time. And it's a beautiful time that we share together, a very sacred space and an awesome gift to give the children. When your children can see you coming from a pure, loving place, it gives them a good example of what relationship is. You are going to have your ups and downs, your crazy moments. You have a hectic life and everything. This is a meditative state that we're in together. It makes the family stronger, more loving, and healthier. Our children like it; they like it a lot.

ONENESS BLESSING IN SCHOOLS

There have also been many schoolteachers from all over the world who have brought the Oneness Blessing back to their classrooms. Linda Van Dien (no relation to Casper) teaches eight-year-olds at a state school in Norway. After the course, she would start her day with the kids by lighting a candle and giving them the Oneness Blessing as a group through intention. The children blossomed, became kinder to each other, assimilated learning more easily, and had more energy. Norway is a very small country, and before long, the local TV showed up in her classroom. The whole class was on TV that night as the first item on the local news. The report was very critical, suggesting that it was a form of religious indoctrination. This eventually sparked a debate throughout the whole country. It was reported in the national newspapers. Linda's principal was courageous and called a meeting of all the parents in the class, together with Linda and the children. The principal determined that if all the parents agreed that it was good for their children, then it could continue. The parents had, indeed, noticed great things happening with their children. The children are happy together now; they look forward to coming to school; they are confident and eager to learn. As a result, the Oneness Blessing continues in the class and also for the parents once a week in the evening. The primary beneficiary, however, has been Linda herself: "I feel I am doing more for children. I have been a teacher for a long time. I feel in my heart that this is the best I can give them, and they can feel this from me. I am glad and smiling more. We are very close now." Similar things have happened in a private school in California, as well as in schools in Germany and Singapore.

Ruthie Grant teaches a critical-thinking class called Life 101 at Los Angeles Mission College in Southern California. She has always been a very popular teacher, and she prides herself on never giving the same lecture twice. Her classes have a three-year waiting list and meet every day for a month.

As soon as Ruthie returned from her training in India, she started to give the Oneness Blessing to groups by intention as she was teaching. "I was seeing a lot of apathy with these students, just not caring that much about anything. When I came back, I immediately noticed a difference in the way that my students reacted to the lectures. I noticed that the students were more open, excited, and perceptive."

Ruthie started a monthly Oneness workshop at her house, where she thought her students would feel safer and more relaxed:

At the first meeting, I had forty students, which is really phenomenal for this campus. Usually you can only get six or eight people to show up for any kind of meeting. The students' responses have just been phenomenal; miraculous things have been happening in their lives.

I've seen this calming of their spirits, this confidence that they have about themselves and about life, wanting to do more and give more and to be an example to others. I've seen them managing work and

school better—they're much more confident about their ability to jug-
gle a lot of things at one time. And they're very, very comfortable in
leadership roles, which they weren't before.

Abraham, for example, is a young Mexican man who has spent a good deal
of his life in violent gang activity and has been in and out of prison. He had
already been pulling his life together for a couple of years before Ruthie came
back from India, and he had become a student math tutor on campus. When
Ruthie described the impact that the Oneness Blessing had on this young
man and his friends, I was curious whether it was evangelical exaggeration and
asked for his phone number. He called me right back.

"During our day, we get bombarded with life. Sometimes things get
tough," Abraham told me on the phone. He went on:

The Oneness Blessing has given me peace of mind. It helps me not let
other people or situations overwhelm me. It clears my mind, and it
helps me concentrate on life's challenges. Every time I get the Blessing, I
walk out like a ball of energy. I know now that there's something going
on that's much larger than just school or work. I don't have to be so
stressed out. I don't have to worry about things. My vision of a well-
spent life is just to have peace of mind, to be happy with myself. Success
to me isn't just about financial needs. It's about looking at yourself in
the mirror and being happy with your life. The Blessing helps us bind
together and understand people. I spend more time listening to oth-
ers. If I can see where their weakness is, I can help take them beyond
that. Leadership is not just leading somebody somewhere; it's helping
somebody actually find out where they want to go.

I have talked to people all over the world who have recovered from addiction or violent lifestyles through the Oneness Blessing and who have gone on to
become leaders and healers for others. Perhaps you remember Johan Mansson,
whose urine showed, after one Blessing, no trace of drug use after sixteen years
of heroin addiction. He has now given his whole life to helping kids get off hard

drugs with the Oneness Blessing. He discovered that the seeds of addiction are created in the womb: "If your mother was sick, disappointed, or in a loveless relationship, you can make a decision while you are still in the womb to say no to life and to yourself. This is the seed of all addiction."

He has been specifically trained by the Oneness University to give a Reborn Blessing, which helps addicts make new decisions. He meets with young people every day in Sweden, but he also gives many of these Blessings for addicts without being physically present. People e-mail him a photo, and he gives them the Blessing anywhere in the world. He asks for no payment, although some people give him gifts in gratitude. "It has such a deep effect," he says. "It really is a miracle. They get jobs and rooms and education. They come out of the hospital, and they can do whatever they want." You can find out how to contact Johan in the Resources section.

The vision of the Oneness University began in a school. When Bhagavan and Amma felt a pull in themselves to do something for the world, they started with youth. Bhagavan says:

We are concerned with creating a new world, building a new kind of human being with a global outlook, who is concerned about the earth and all that is happening on the planet. We thought youth would be the best bet for this. Hence this tremendous focus on youth, so that they can emerge as new human beings, very different from whatever was there earlier.

In one of our interviews for this book, I asked Bhagavan what he would say to young people all over the world, if he had a chance to give them one simple message. Here was his reply:

I would say you have to discover love in your life. Unconditional love! That would be my message—because that is what youth really want. They are not getting it from their parents; they are not getting it from their teachers; they are not getting it from the society. Through deeksha, they can discover that love. They are not beggars, waiting to receive love; they are those who can give love. They can discover love within themselves. At the Oneness University, we see children receiving love from within themselves, which they then give to their parents. And the parents also get transformed. I have more hope in the children than in their parents.

CHAPTER EIGHT

THE ONENESS BLESSING
AND ART

Angelica Schiffer has been a musician all her life. For the past eighteen years, singing and playing sacred devotional music has been her passion. The homemade instruments she plays—all built by a close friend—are like nothing you have seen before. One of them has strings on both sides—fifty all together—making it a tambura, a monochord, and a koto all in one. She recorded her first CD at home and gave it away to friends, selling a few here and there. She would play occasional concerts, but music always stayed a hobby while she supported herself with her catering business. By the summer of 2005, no new material had come through for several years, and she felt things were running dry. That was when she attended a two-day Oneness retreat:

> *Right afterward, I was doing an out-of-town catering job, up in Lake Tahoe. I was living there, working fourteen hours a day, but even so, these songs were coming to me—improvisations on mantras I already knew, as well as completely new songs. So, after a full day of work, between midnight and three in the morning, I was recording the songs that came. I set up my digital recorder in the closet and recorded half a CD in a few days. When inspiration comes, you can't wait; you have to follow. I was so exhausted, I said, "God, you sing; I am too tired to sing." These pieces are the best of the whole album.*

Angelica and her partner went to India soon after, and since then, music has been her full-time job. She has recorded three more albums in a year, done several concert tours, supported herself completely with her music, and paid off the debts that her music was previously creating. The way that Angelica's creative process has opened is typical for artists from many media whose work has been impacted by the Oneness Blessing. As she says:

> *I relax my body and mind, and I empty out. Then I simply reach out to . . . I don't know where. Maybe the universe? When I am in receiving mode, all the usual parts of me that are in charge of day-to-day life get out of the way. In a way, it's a prayer, but with an answer. It's a conversation with the universe. I sit with the instruments quietly, and then something comes and I hear it in my head. I sing it as I hear it. Often it is a completely finished melody. My next step is to learn it. I have to record it because I do not know it by heart already. Often I can just record the final version then and there into my digital hard drive, which is like a little sound studio in a box. Often I don't need to edit at all. With my song "Kyrie Eleison," for example, I didn't do anything. I closed my eyes and attuned myself with love. I just sang, and it came out. I never made any changes or edits.*

Tamara Tavernier illustrates and writes children's books. She used to complete one new book every year; now she finishes a project in a month:

> *I just start. I don't think. I take my pencil in my hand, and I just know which colors to use. I just have to follow this guidance from within. I just have to ask, "Which image now?" Then comes a bear or a dolphin, and I never know why. I just do it. Then I'm in a flow, and the rest comes.*

INVOKING THE PRESENCE

Most of the artists whose work has been transformed by the Oneness Blessing describe how they consciously open themselves to the divine before they begin to create or perform. They most often call this "invoking the presence." Anandagiri explains:

To really excel in anything—be it art, science, engineering, math, anything at all—if there is excellence, God is there. The more you can open yourself to the presence and the more you allow the presence to flow through you, the greater it will be. Of course, people are born with specific gifts, like art or business. But for it to really flower, for you to really fulfill your destiny, you must come in touch with grace and establish a connection with presence. Very consciously, we can make this happen. Nahuel calls it "wings of grace." Suddenly he feels grace coming. When grace is coming, he goes into music. He goes on playing and records it because he does not know if he can do it again. So there's a moment for him to record it. He'll be waiting, and it comes. If he can compose then, that's an excellent piece.

Nahuel Schajris first met Anandagiri when they were both in their teens. Nahuel's mother met Bhagavan and the dasas in the mid-1990s, when she was making a documentary film in India. She was so touched by them that she invited Anandagiri to visit her family in Argentina. As soon as the young monk arrived, he formed a bond with her son Nahuel. They were around the same age. Later, when Nahuel had a place of his own, Anandagiri would stay in his apartment. "I developed a great friendship with Anandagiri," recalls Nahuel. "I suddenly felt like he was my brother, he was my teacher, he was the best friend in the whole world. That was the first experience for me, the experience of real friendship with someone." When Anandagiri came to town, Nahuel would go out in the evening and play music in the local bars and restaurants to make enough for them to eat. The tips were just enough to feed the two of them the next day. Later, Nahuel traveled to India and met Bhagavan and Amma in person for the first time. "I love music," he told Bhagavan, who at that point had not yet met many Westerners, especially as young as Nahuel. "I think music can help share the message of awakening and Oneness to reach more people. I think I could be a good instrument to share all this in a good way." Bhagavan looked quizzically at Nahuel. "You think music can help to spread awakening?" There was a silence. "Okay," he said, "let's do it."

As soon as Nahuel returned home, he found he could easily invoke the presence to write songs. He formed a partnership with his friend Leo to write songs for other artists. Bhagavan had given Nahuel specific "auspicious" dates, down to the hour, when he should invoke the presence and write. They wrote thirty songs in one and a half months. Things did not work out so well selling these songs to other artists, so instead they created their own band, Sin Bandera. Their first album was signed by Sony and has now sold two million copies. They have recorded three more albums since then and won the Latin Grammy two years in a row.

Nahuel speaks of invoking presence constantly, in his composing as well as in their concerts, which often bring fifty thousand people. He describes the process of composing:

I know, "Okay, now is the moment. Something is coming." I feel like it is the right moment to sit and play the guitar or the piano and to receive something. I don't know how it works, really. When I am there, music stops. When I am not there, music flows. That's all there is to it. If the mind is there, the music stops, because the nature of mind is to judge, to compare, to label. When mind is involved, art loses something. When you are there, mind is there. When you are not there, mind stops working. The mind can't control the process of creation. It comes at unexpected times. I just know that I have to sit with an instrument in my hand. Something comes, and I record it and let it be there. Then I come back later, I hear it, and, wow, I'm amazed at the beauty.

The Oneness Blessing has rewired my brain in a way that changed my heart. I'm more open now to feel the universe and all the things that surround me. That vulnerability is wonderful, because I am more in touch with everything around me. It's like a radio that works better. I receive more radio stations now. It's not my music; it's the universe's music. It's there, and I channel it. I tune in to a specific broadcast and

a specific musical idea, and I receive it, and I express it through my
filters and through my radio. The Oneness Blessing cleaned my radio,
put it in very sharp and powerful tuning.

His wife, Karla Goudinoff, is a writer, photographer, poet, and dancer. She
remembers the way that mind would sabotage her work:

I have been writing since I was ten or eleven years old. But I did not
believe that it had any value, so I would quit in the middle. I thought
it had no value to anyone. Then I stopped writing completely. I took a
job in advertising. The Oneness Blessing opened a channel—just like
you turn on the shower and out comes the water. I could not stop writ-
ing, all day long. I kept a notebook with me and filled two of them in
three weeks. There was a frog in our bedroom when we visited India.
I filled a whole notebook just with the teachings of that frog.

Anandagiri explains that this kind of invocation can turn any part of life
into a work of art:

You can invoke the presence for your painting, for your dance, for
your music, for writing, for poetry, for anything. There are people
who invoke presence in sports—in cricket, for example. There are so
many surgeons who have been touched in this way. They might have
a patient with problems and complications and not know what to
do. Through deeksha, you get in touch with the divine, and you start
excelling, because that is the supreme intelligence.

THE ~~STARVING~~ THRIVING ARTIST

We are so used to the image of the impoverished artist, the tortured soul
who never sees their work appreciated in their own lifetime and dies without
ever knowing if their gift will be received. Van Gogh died still in debt to his
brother. Mozart died in abject poverty, as did William Blake and Ludwig van

Beethoven. The Oneness Blessing seems to break that mold. Nahuel got contracts with Sony and won a couple of Grammys. Angelica is out of debt and selling CDs like hotcakes at her concerts.

We met Venkatesh Balasubramanian in the previous chapter on youth. He is Jaya's husband. He got his master's degree in fine arts, but he was never able to support himself through his art because it never made enough money to pay the bills. Once he and Jaya got married and had a child, the artist's life seemed even more remote. He created a successful career in a software company, assuming his art would become no more than a hobby. At an exhibition of the art of alumni from his college, former students showed their work. As Venkatesh describes it, most of his former classmates were very shy, almost apologetic about their work. There was a press conference, and no one wanted to talk about their art—except for Venkatesh, who had recently completed his youth deeksha course. "I was never able to speak this confidently before. I was really fearful. If you asked me a question, my throat would contract and all kinds of fears would come up. Now, as you can see, I'm relieved of that fear."

A few weeks later, a representative of the World Bank contacted him. They were creating a new headquarters in India and needed artwork throughout the building. The vice president invited Venkatesh into the bank, looked at his work, and immediately ordered seventeen paintings, two bronze sculptures, and a mural, seven feet by four feet. The World Bank had plenty of other bidders and usually never gave any project like this to an outside vendor—all their contracts were with previously registered contractors. The vice president said that he felt inexplicably happy looking at Venkatesh's paintings, so he made an exception. Now Venkatesh has the freedom to become a full-time artist. This has been the trend with artists all over the world, in every medium, who have received the Oneness Blessing. Not only does their art flow more easily, but it also mutates more easily into cash when required.

CROSSING THE BOUNDARIES OF MEDIA

Other than a few projects as an art student, Venkatesh has primarily worked in oils on canvas. Once he began receiving deeksha, as it is still known in India, he started to expand beyond the familiar boundaries of his medium. He found he was able to draw with pen and ink. When the offer came from the World Bank for the sculptures and the mural, he did not hesitate for one moment. "I don't ask anymore if I can do this. So much confidence has built up in the presence. I know the presence can do it through me." The sculptures are in bronze and each is more than three feet tall; the mural he is designing is in mixed media, a bronze sheet with thousands of copper wires. He accepted the contract with no idea of what he would do and no previous experience with works of this size.

Venkatesh has noticed his maturation as an artist accelerating in other ways, too. He has been aware, both in himself and with other artists, of milestones in his work:

We artists will often do paintings in a series—a nature series, for example. We do thirty paintings in that series, and then we start a new series. A phase like this might last for six months or a year. There is a feeling of passing a milestone when a series is completed, then you start another series with another maturity level. These days, that feeling of a milestone comes with every painting. The level of satisfaction, the feeling of having done what I wanted to achieve, the feeling of being able to move to another level, which I used to have maybe once a year, I now feel painting after painting.

Karla Goudinoff is just completing her first book. It is about the goddess Aphrodite, the Greek goddess of love. The book is for women all over the world. It includes Karla's photographs, her poetry, and her prose writing. She has divided the book into many parts. The first is called "Mind," and it is a dialogue between Aphrodite and contemporary women. The second part is called "Soul," and it contains her devotional poetry to Aphrodite. The last part is called "Body," containing photos of drops of water on different parts of the body. Many other artists touched by the Oneness Blessing simultaneously work in multiple media in this way. Many say that they now see that the restriction to one medium was an identification in the mind only and that the presence they now invoke works in all media at the same time.

BLESSINGS THROUGH ART

Artists in every medium discover that not only is their work a way to express beauty, but the art they create in this spirit of divine invocation becomes a form of Blessing in and of itself. When Rick Allen, the drummer of Def Leppard, became a Blessing giver, he wanted to share the Oneness Blessing with others—but not by having to explain it and touch their heads. He asked Bhagavan and the dasas for the ability to give very strong Blessings through his drumming and his voice. Let's not spoil the surprise by telling you the result here. Buy tickets to a Def Leppard concert and find out for yourself. Promise? Okay.

The popular singers Deva Premal and Miten, whose collections of devotional mantras have sold close to a million copies, give the Oneness Blessing in their concerts—as do Maneesh de Moor and Sudha, Angelica, and Nahuel. Catherine Oxenberg and her husband, Casper Van Dien, say that people can feel the Oneness Blessing coming through their acting roles. "After I was on television last week," says Catherine, "I got dozens of calls from friends saying that they saw light pouring off me. Golden light. I have not had that happen before." The couple went on *Larry King Live* together to talk about their work with survivors of sexual abuse, and the same thing happened. Catherine says:

> Now I only want to do projects that are permeated with presence. I have asked myself my entire life, "Did I miss my life's calling? Why didn't I choose to marry a prince and live a cushy, predictable life?" [Prince Andrew did, in fact, propose to her at Buckingham Palace the night of Charles and Diana's wedding.] Why did I choose this insane calling to be an actress, which is such a hellish life? It is full of rejection, it's unpredictable, and it has so many other downsides. I would say, "God, if you gave me this calling, then fulfill it!" I feel, with the Oneness Blessing, the energy comes through me on the screen. I've prayed, and I asked for the Blessing to come through my voice, through my eyes, through my body—both for Casper and for me—so that whatever we do, we have the power to transform and uplift people through our presence.

CHAPTER NINE

THE ONENESS BLESSING
AND BUSINESS

Jitendra Mohanty owns the Swosti Group, in the state of Orissa in India. With a staff of nine hundred, he operates three five-star hotels, a convention center, a beach resort, and an international travel agency. A small man, invariably dressed in a pinstripe suit and a silk tie, there is nothing remotely "fringe" about Mr. Mohanty. Trained at Cornell, he has won a variety of business awards, including Hotel Entrepreneur of the Year from the Federation of Hotel and Restaurant Association of India. He started his chain from scratch in 1984 and has given over his life, body, and soul to it ever since. For a man like Mr. Mohanty, success in business has been his reason to live. Failure has never been an option.

And so it was that when room occupancy went down and Mr. Mohanty had to go into significant debt to stay afloat, he took the change of circumstances very badly. His sleep suffered, his health was affected by stress, and he found himself snapping at his family. Hitting rock bottom, he was ready to try anything new. He laid off some staff, looked for new managers, and explored the latest and greatest business models. But nothing helped. Then, one weekend, he got a visit from his old friend Rajiv Mishra, an exporter of seafood to Europe. Rajiv's business had also been through rocky times, until he took off on some kind of a spiritual course. In one year, everything turned around, to the point that he was making enough profit to invest elsewhere. As far as Mr. Mohanty was concerned, things could not get any worse for him and his family. Although more drawn to a Yale business course than a yoga ashram, he called the number his friend had given him, and found himself talking to a young monk called Namann. "No problem," said the monk casually, after listening to Mr. Mohanty's litany of woes. "Come here for three days and do a Oneness course, and we can set your business right." Little did Mr. Mohanty and his wife, Bipasa, know what was in store for them. They traveled to the Oneness University and took the course under Namann's guidance. On the last day, they met with Bhagavan to ask his blessings on the business, as is traditional in India. Bhagavan told them that things would certainly get better after their visit, but for the full shebang, it would be better to come back for a twenty-one-day Oneness Process. Sure enough, things began to pick up as soon as they got home, and a month later, they were back for what they expected to be advanced business training. Mr. Mohanty was surprised:

The dasa would come in the morning, and he would say, "Today we will give a healing for your mind." After two minutes, he would leave, and we would lie down and feel very relaxed. As soon as he left, our heads would start reeling. Something was happening. For two days, we both had headaches. But then, tremendous peace followed. They explained this was the "surgery" that was needed. "Surgery?" we asked. "What kind of surgery?" We were both laughing behind their backs; we did not believe what they were saying. I am a businessman trained at Cornell! But there were so many highly educated people from the United States and Europe there: bishops, Muslim leaders, Hindu leaders, university professors, doctors, lecturers. We thought that all these people could not be wrong. So we followed the directions anyway. Then another day, he came and said, "Now we will do a deeksha to heal your body."

"There is nothing wrong with my body," I explained to him.

"You don't know what is wrong with your body," he said. "Neither do we. But the divine power will take care of everything." For the next two days, every part of our bodies was aching.

For three weeks, it went on like this. They had deeksha (as it is still called in India) for the relationship with their mothers, their fathers, their ancestors. They felt all the pain they had caused to others, and all the pain they had stuffed in themselves. Mr. and Mrs. Mohanty got a total workout—everything you can imagine, except the strategies for running a hotel, for which they were waiting. From time to time, Mr. Mohanty got worried about his hotels, how they were doing in his absence. He had not left them for more than three days since 1984. The dasas had told him to put away his mobile phone and his laptop and to leave the running of the hotel to the divine. He and his wife slept a lot, took walks, and experienced deep healings on inner planes. Sometimes he would sneak in a phone call to his manager at eleven at night—it was always good news. The staff was happy; long-time debts had gotten settled; business had increased. Something was happening that had not been covered in his training at Cornell. Everything was going more smoothly than when he was physically present at the hotel. "After I came out from those twenty-one days," he reports, "my business tension and depression had all gone. I was very positive, very optimistic. Since then, business has improved tremendously."

Before Mr. and Mrs. Mohanty left the Oneness University, where they also became deeksha givers, they had a final meeting with Bhagavan. They were so impressed with everything that had happened for them that they wanted all their employees, as well as the employees' families, to also experience deeksha. If Namann could come to Orissa to give deeksha, they would organize a huge event. Bhagavan told them, "Namann will come, but he will not give deeksha. You and your wife will give deeksha in the hotel. Namann will introduce you, because your employees should not misunderstand that their boss has gone to some spiritual place and become a guru or a spiritual master. Namann will clear up any misunderstanding, and then you will give deeksha. I want to show them that normal people like you, heads of organizations, can also give deeksha, can also have spiritual powers. It is not just the prerogative of only a few spiritual masters."

And so it happened. All the employees gathered, with their families and children—more than two thousand people. Namann spoke, and then the CEO and his wife gave deeksha to everyone there. In India, the culture makes it much easier for people to have mystical visions. So some people in that first event saw images of deities; some saw their ancestors; some experienced tremendous silence. The next day, the phones were busy all day with excitement. Some reported that they had slept soundly for the first time in many months.

Mr. and Mrs. Mohanty have sponsored five more events like this in their convention center. Together with the twenty other local deeksha givers, they have now given deeksha to more than four thousand people. Every day, Mr. Mohanty maintains an open-door policy in his office. Any of his staff, from the managers to the cooks to the people who sweep the floors, can come to receive deeksha from him or his wife. Their families are welcome, too. They give one hundred to two hundred deekshas a day. Not every employee took to this like ducks to water. One of the top managers, for example, worried that the deeksha conflicted with his religious beliefs. He was actually organizing the large deeksha events at the convention center but not taking the deeksha himself. After some months, he found another job. There have been a few others like this who have moved on of their own accord, such that now all the nine hundred staff are regularly receiving deeksha.

Mr. Mohanty's hotel chain is an example of a small but growing number of businesses that have openly embraced deeksha. Bhagavan sees the head of every business as having the potential to be not just an administrator but also a kind of spiritual leader. Indeed, Mr. Mohanty says he now has a completely new kind of relationship with his staff. He knows them all in a personal way; they have a new kind of bond. They look to him and his wife as family, with affection and devotion. As a result, his employees are much more dedicated to their work. Three months after the introduction of deeksha, staff turnover reduced to almost zero. Absenteeism has gone down to less than 10 percent of its previous levels. The quality of service has improved so much that, in just a few months, all three hotels had and still have close to 100 percent occupancy. The chain's annual revenue has nearly doubled, allowing Mr. Mohanty to increase salaries across the board to the highest levels in the industry. He is in the process of opening three new hotels. He explains:

Everybody has a very strong self-confidence about them now. Today there is so much of a crowd of guests coming and so much business, you find the staff running around smartly, smiling at everybody, and do-ing a good job. They are all on their toes. It is an internal change that has occurred. Those employees who were not efficient left of their own accord; I did not fire a single person. My staff hardly needs any supervision now; they're on their own. Even if somebody is doing something wrong, five other staff will tell them about it. Matters are solved at their level; it doesn't come up to me. There is such a positive change all around. I don't have to do much of anything anymore.

THE GIGGLING MONK

Namann was thirteen years old when he enrolled as the very first student at the Jeevashram school in 1984. Even today, you can still see the exuberant nine-year-old boy in him. His dimpled cheeks and contagious enthusiasm give him a cherubic quality. It's easier to envision him on a spending spree at the toy store than in the boardrooms of some of India's biggest companies. But after finishing at the Jeevashram school with Bhagavan, Namann went on to study chartered accountancy, and he now shares deeksha in India's corporate world.

We have been taught to choose between money and God. Most religious traditions maintain that if you are going to pursue profit and business and success, you can forget all about the spiritual life; if you really want the divine, you must give up the world. For the dasas at the Oneness University, like Namann and Anandagiri, this distinction does not exist. "Most companies consider spirituality out of place for them," says Namann. "But this is only because they do not know what true spirituality is. In the corporate sector, they want to achieve their financial targets. They want to increase the efficiency of human resources, which is what we do at Oneness University. We customize and tailor our programs to each company's requirements."

Sitting behind his large CEO-style desk in his leather swivel chair, Namann got more and more excited as we talked. His spacious office reminded me of the executive suite of a large corporation: the flat-screen monitor, the decor that had obviously required a top-class designer, the concealed lighting, the embossed stationery. And right there, in the middle of it all, was a bubbly monk hardly able to contain his excitement for the ecstatic union of commerce and communion with the divine. He says:

A person who is unhappy is going to be a danger to society as well as to a company. He is going to be a danger to the organization, because internally he is one thing and externally he's something else. That hypocrisy will destroy the person and the organization itself. If the individual is not happy, then the company is not going to succeed. We work on that internal aspect. As long as each person does not accept themselves, there will be a struggle.

Anandagiri chimes in:

We see so much crime, war, conflict, fear, terror, poverty, so many problems in the world. What do you think will make a real difference—somebody meditating out on the hills? Is that going to make a difference? What will make a difference to this world are really happy people. We're talking about happiness, not pleasure. If someone is truly happy, he will be such an asset to society and to a company that he will create wealth. A happy person cannot but cause happiness to others; a happy person can only share. Spirituality is about happiness. If you can be truly happy, you are spiritual. Spirituality is drinking a glass of water and experiencing it totally. When the quality of your everyday experience changes, simple day-to-day events—like talking to people, driving your car, working on your computer, watching a movie, or eating a pizza—become sacred. When you can experience these things totally, the quality of that experience changes, and that is spirituality.

I was starting to wonder how all this would translate into a living reality. How do you make the people in a corporation truly happy in a one-and-a-half day seminar? Does it require clown noses? Balloons? Steve Martin movies? I wanted to know what, exactly, Namann does in the executive suite. "It's not just teachings," he explained:

The higher energies that come through the Oneness deeksha make teachings into a reality. When we start, they are often stuck in problems and not able to move forward. Work is not happening, and the company goes into loss. Once the senior executives get clear inside themselves, more relaxed, outside things automatically start happening in a big way. That is what the deeksha does. I have seen many cases where, during the break from our session, an executive will get a phone call reporting good news; the problem they had been so concerned about was solved.

Namann remembers one of the programs he offered at a large factory. The general manager and twenty-five senior officers of the plant took two days off from work to be with Namann, who told them to relax, to forget about work, and to hand everything over to grace. Then the general manager received an urgent page that the plant was in danger. The alarm had gone off; people were in a panic. It was a decisive moment, a test almost. He had already done other Oneness programs with Namann at their national office, he had already tasted what is possible, so he was willing to take a risk. In this case, a big risk. Instead of answering the page, he received a Oneness deeksha and invoked the divine to take care of the situation. Then he relaxed totally. He got no more pages that day, but in the evening he called and found that the problem had righted itself just at the time when he received the deeksha and invoked divine grace. "Now," says Namann, "he is able to handle all kinds of situations in a new way. He has a new confidence because he no longer feels alone. The Oneness deeksha has given him connection to higher energy."

To a Western mind like mine, stories like this seem almost ridiculous—exaggeration, fabrication, or random coincidence. Initially I planned to exclude them from this book, for fear I would never get published again. It was only after I heard these kinds of reports over and over—and not only from dozens of Indian executives, but also from businesspeople in China, Europe, and the United States—that I began to think something was going on that is not explained in business school.

I still wanted to know more from Namann about what all this looks like. Indian businesspeople manage to be even more corporate then their Western counterparts. Stick twenty-five pillars of corporate correctness in a room with one very excited and somewhat divinely intoxicated monk, and what do you get? I really wanted to know.

Namann's one-and-a-half day seminar is divided into several modules. The first focuses on the quality of relationship within the company. "A company is not unlike a family," says Namann:

> If the relationships within the company are not right, then the company will break down and collapse. Let us say a production manager and a marketing manager have had some differences. Perhaps they have personal grudges, such as "He insulted me in front of the board," or "He would not respect what I said." Ultimately, because the relationship is not right, other major decisions will be going wrong. There has to be real forgiveness, which means really feeling the pain that has been caused and the pain we have caused others. They have not forgiven, and they have not experienced. We help them with that.

Namann shared with me that they also work with breathing exercises. He maintains that most people in a business environment are breathing in a very controlled way, which affects the way they make decisions. They also work with posture.

"But all these things are less than 5 percent of it," he says:

> Ninety-five percent is the Oneness deeksha. While they are contemplating their relationships, or practicing new ways of breathing or new posture, I am silently giving them deeksha. Every day, I also give them each hands-on deeksha. Then they feel not only relaxed in the body but also tremendously relaxed in the mind. If we only did the exercises, it would be just another stress management program. It happens on a much deeper level.

Namann has brought this unique cocktail to many of India's biggest corporations. Godrej & Boyce is the largest manufacturer of appliances in India.

Anil Mathur is the chief operating officer of the furniture division. He reports that, simply through his own experience of Oneness deeksha, the efficiency of his entire division has increased. He says he can depend on an inner connection for the right decision, rather than have to think everything through. And the decision always turns out to be smarter, better informed, and more creative than thinking it through. Similar stories have come from legal firms, media companies, doctors, government agencies, and universities whose management have taken Namann's courses.

"The only thing that is emphasized is the Oneness deeksha itself," says Mr. Mohanty. He continues:

> You get more and more Oneness deeksha and give more and more deeksha, and the rest happens automatically. It is a transfer of positive energy. The more you pass it on, the more you have. It helps society, it helps the business, and it helps every individual. This will be very difficult for the rest of the world to understand, I know. I travel to the West. I visit Europe and the United States. I have friends everywhere. It is very difficult to explain this to the Western world.

Despite this difficulty, the same kinds of results are just starting to happen in the West.

BUSINESS AS LOVE

One Western businessman who seemed to have very little trouble understanding the power of the Oneness Blessing was Geert Timan, the owner and CEO of Limburg Patisserie BV, a quality bakery in southern Holland that has been in his family since 1945. It started out just catering to the local villages but has grown to be the biggest company of its kind in Europe, selling to more than sixty international airlines as well as restaurants throughout Europe. In the late 1990s, Geert went through a midlife crisis. "I couldn't understand what it was all about," he says. "Making money, getting a car, getting a bigger car, getting a house, getting a bigger house, and so on. I thought, 'There must be more to life,' and I started to search." Geert learned meditation, attended various teachings, and ended up in India, becoming a Oneness Blessing giver.

The most important way the Oneness Blessing has affected my business is that it has transformed it into a business fueled by love. My clients and I are in a state of consciousness that is fully in this present moment and that is fully carried by love. As you know, business is not always a matter of love. But that's how I experience it. As soon as I am not attached to anything—not even the product I want to sell—the feeling becomes even stronger. It is so wonderful to be talking about business with a layer of love from the start. It opens doors, because when people feel good with you, it makes even the cakes that we are selling more tasty.

Wow.

And here I was, thinking Namann was way out there.

Geert told me of a recent meeting he had with a team from one of the world's biggest airlines. I'd love to tell you the name, but he suggested I don't. Once you hear the story, you'll understand why. A team of eight executives came to arrange a deal to buy cake from Geert's company. (Why did they send eight executives to sign a cake deal? Must be the free samples.) As soon as they were settled into the meeting and relaxed, Geert began giving his clients the Oneness Blessing through his eyes. "You know, Geert, your building has such a wonderful feeling," one of the executives commented. "It is four hundred years old, isn't it?" Sometimes Geert explains that it is more than the building, and sometimes he just lets it go. He says he only explains if someone asks him directly.

The conversation got better and deeper. At a certain point, Geert reports, some of the executives started to tear up with pure happiness. The meeting went on for hours; no one wanted to end it.

"Finally, they got up to leave," he said. "And they hugged me. Why would these businessmen hug me? They are not used to hugging each other."

The next day, the senior managing director called to give Geert the biggest contract in the company's history. But he did not fax it or mail it; instead, he did the six-hour round-trip all over again and hand-delivered it. "Geert," he said, "it feels wonderful to be with you again. It feels like you don't have any problems at all. You're always laughing and funny—happiness itself." Upon reading it, Geert saw that the contract had an unusual clause, stipulating frequent meetings with Geert, exactly like the one they had the day before. He laughed, and told them they did not need to write this in the contract; they were always welcome to come and visit, like family.

Sooner or later, Geert's clients ask him for his secret. They usually start out casually. What kind of books do you read? Are you on any kind of a special diet? What is your favorite skin cream? Then their eyes narrow and they zero in: "I heard that you've been to India recently. What did you learn there?" Only then does Geert explain about the Oneness Blessing and the relationship he has built with Amma and Bhagavan. He offers to give them a hands-on Blessing. He tells me that he never pushes it. If they feel it already and if they ask, then he tells them. Many of his clients now come back just for the Blessing. "They come back more often. Sometimes they cannot come here, so they call me for a Blesssing over the phone. I love, and I give. There is no competition; there is no anger; there is only love."

Geert explains that this shifting to love as his only agenda has affected every aspect of the business. Business language becomes more effective; he needs fewer and simpler words to come to the same final result. He gets much bigger and more frequent orders. Limburg Patisserie has seen a 40 percent increase in revenue in the eight months following Geert's trip to India. Their factory has increased from one shift to two and is now increasing again to three. They are building a second plant.

There are relatively few businesspeople in the Western world who use the Oneness Blessing in their businesses as openly as Geert does, although hundreds of Western business leaders have been trained to give Blessings. Most keep it to themselves, for fear of seeming cultish or crazy and losing business in a culture that is not known for embracing spirituality in the workplace.

CHANGE FROM WITHIN

Alice Lee is another courageous Oneness Blessing pioneer, in Taiwan. She completed her master's degree in Beijing, so she also has close ties to China. She is the owner of Alice Lee, Inc., and Plenty More. She manufactures medical instrument parts and isotope reagents for use in nuclear medicine for distribution all over the world. It was when she was offered new opportunities in China that she started to feel limited in herself. "This is something really big," she told me. "I felt I did not have enough power within me to handle this new challenge. My ancestry is Chinese," she told me. "I was educated in China, and now China has become the economic hope of the whole world. I am a Buddhist, and I was seeking some insight from the Guiding Buddha, a female deity. I think that she guided me to the Oneness Blessing."

Before her Oneness Process, Alice had significant challenges in her office. "I had a very bad temper before. I was a very bossy, dominating, and demanding woman. I was the kind of person who couldn't wait till people had finished talking before I would just cut in and tell everybody what I think, what I want. I never listened."

There are two departments in Alice's office: one for overseeing the manufacturing and one in charge of orders and distribution. Each has a director who reports to her. The two directors were always fighting with each other. Alice felt conflicted, because they were both very capable. She knew she would have to get rid of one of them, because they hated each other so much—but which one?

Alice initially went to India for fourteen days. She was amazed to find that while she was away, the two directors started sorting out their differences. By the time she got back, they were getting along quite well, cooperating to handle clients and to solve problems. "I don't know why," says Alice, "but they have totally changed. It's like they are completely new people. I used to have to lecture them, to tell them my ideas in great detail. Now they catch on without my saying too much."

She gives the Oneness Blessing to her entire office staff once a month and to the two directors every ten days or so. She tries to do so on a Friday, as they invariably go home and fall asleep for two days. Alice reports that her revenue has increased by one-third in the five months after her first trip to India.

While Alice was still debating the opportunities in China, she went back to Beijing for a college reunion. Two of her classmates were children of two of the governors of China. "They both approached me. They say they felt something different about me, a brightness in my face. We ended up becoming very close, like sisters. Later, I found out that my friend's father, one of the governors, is supervising the department where my project in China is planned. All of this happened without my conscious doing."

This type of experience is repeated among business leaders all over the world who receive Oneness Blessings: they see greater results by doing less. Ray Butler is a British property developer. With his partners, he buys apartment and office buildings in central London, remodels them extensively, and then resells them to investors. "I have always been very driven," says Ray. "I am like one of these very fast French trains, roaring along. It's not allowed to get off, stop and look around, much less play, relax, or have fun. I've been roaring along all my life." Ray describes himself as having been a perpetual list writer: big lists with hundreds of things on them. As soon as a few get checked off, others rush in to fill their places.

Ray and his wife, Marie, bought Penninghame House, in Scotland, some years ago and turned it into a retreat center. Through the different courses being offered, they came to hear about the Oneness Blessing, and both went for the training in India. "I don't do lists anymore," says Ray:

I don't even do much planning. I address what happens each day and what comes up. It is a different approach. I think I was making myself busy where I didn't need to be. I get much more done, and I have more time for myself. I am a human being now; I'm not a human doing anymore. I let things happen. I don't think about it; it just happens. I deal with this; I deal with that:

Marie feels the shift, too:

He does a third of what he used to, and his business is getting bigger and bigger. I can't explain that. Perhaps he is more focused now; he

eliminated a lot of needless things. All of a sudden, I have a husband
who is around more, with a normal family life, and at the same time
with a business that is growing very, very fast.

Every time I listened to another story like Ray and Marie's, I wondered
how to explain it to the Western businesspeople I know. Most of them are
running around all day with cell phones and Palm Pilots, BlackBerries and
blueberries, and a packed agenda. Slowing down and allowing things to happen seems a far-off dream to most executives. So I asked Ray, "How would
you explain, to regular businesspeople, that slowing down is the way to increase business? Most people are afraid that if they stop, their business will
flounder." Ray replied:

I'd say it's all a viewpoint. When one looks at it, everything is happening
on its own. Who is really the doer of any of it, anyway? What is really go-
ing on here? I'd say that it is an illusion that we are the doer. Things have
their own way of unfolding. I can understand why some people might be
worried that if you slow down, you won't achieve as much. For us, it has
been quite the opposite. There are two ways to explain that. Part of it is
cumulative: the history, the fact that we have been at it twenty-some-odd
years, built a good reputation, and so on. That's one obvious conclusion
you could have. The other is hard to define. It has been extraordinary for
us. Suddenly, we found ourselves at a point where things aren't problems
anymore. We used to struggle all the time, but then it became very easy,
indeed, and big figures rolled in without any effort.

Bhagavan sees that business can be a sacred pursuit and in no way at odds
with spiritual life. He has encouraged many people, including me and most
of my friends, to abandon their Gandhi-esque thinking and to pursue wealth
with greater passion:

Prosperity and poverty are dependent on the mind-set of the individual.
If your thinking is defective, it will result in failure and disorder. People

who worship poverty and have a wrong understanding of detachment ruin their lives. A spiritual person is often supposed to be otherworldly and is expected to express contempt for money and material prosperity. Let me tell you: to create wealth and to succeed, by itself, is a spiritual sadhana, *given that it needs a focused mind, creativity, and hard work. If people would realize that creating wealth and sharing it with others is an extraordinary spiritual activity, they would become much happier and would be responsible for creating a better world.*

CHAPTER TEN

THE ONENESS BLESSING
AND SOCIETY

If you had driven into the small town of Varadaiahpalem as recently as 2002, it would not have seemed a likely candidate for a model society. In the back country of Andhra Pradesh, after you turn off the main highway from Chennai to Calcutta, it is halfway to . . . nowhere at all. This was rural India at its most basic: Many houses were mud huts with no running water, electricity, or sewage. Entire families would live and sleep in one room. Cooking was done on a kerosene stove outside. The bathroom was the nearest field. The small population of seven thousand had tremendous social problems, from rampant alcoholism to spousal abuse. The local police station of fifteen constables, which served the *mandal,* or district, was busy every day breaking up drunken fights in the street. Unemployment was around 40 percent. Children born here had very few opportunities, and many grew into bitter and restless adolescents. The local school was one of the worst in the state, leaving the town's teenagers with few prospects for work or education.

When Bhagavan and the dasas moved to land near Varadaiahpalem, they decided to "adopt" a few villages, inviting them to become like a family. They were ready in the long term to help with medical attention, education, and employment, but Bhagavan knew that all those things would be no good unless people also knew how to be happy. "From the beginning," says Anandagiri, "Bhagavan told us that the index of development in a community is happiness. If you can create truly happy people, that will lead to all the other changes in the village. You will create happy communities by helping people to improve their relationships."

When Anandagiri started to offer classes in the nearby villages with some of the other dasas, they met with great resistance. On the way to the first class in the rickshaw, they saw three different drunken fights in the streets. The people said, "We are not interested in some new philosophy or religion. We are not interested in your classes in improving our relationships. Give us homes. Give us clean water. Give us electricity. Give us hospitals and schools." They were angry. They wanted to chase these intruders out of town. But Anandagiri stood firm. "First, let's work on these deeper aspects of your life. Otherwise, no matter what you have, you will still feel unhappy, and your life will still seem meaningless." Finally, about thirty or forty people from all the surrounding areas took Anandagiri's advice, attended regular weekly classes with the dasas, and received Oneness deeksha, as it is known in India. Once a month, they would come for a free, full-weekend course.

It did not take long for things to change for these first villagers who came to Anandagiri's classes. It was mostly women attending, but their entire families felt the change. Up until this time, home was a place of conflict for most of the villagers. Suddenly, these same families wanted to spend time together. Drinking and spousal abuse became less and less a problem.

These first families started bringing more and more people to the classes and to deeksha. Today, classes and Oneness deeksha events are conducted every night, somewhere in the local area, with as many as a thousand people attending each event.

This phenomenon has evolved into what is now known as the "Hundred Village Project." The idea came from the villagers themselves, and Bhagavan and the dasas readily agreed. It is actually a misnomer, because the project includes closer to 140 villages. All are found within a radius of twelve to fifteen kilometers around Varadaiahpalem. Not everyone in each village is involved or even interested. At the first gathering of the project, attendance was fewer than a thousand people. By June 2006, a meeting brought more than six thousand. These simple and almost entirely uneducated villagers share a common vision: to create communities that are truly happy, that demonstrate higher consciousness at a collective level. An estimated twenty thousand villagers have now received Oneness deeksha, which equals approximately 20 percent of the total population in the area.

Back in the 1970s, Lyall Watson wrote a book called *The Romeo Error*. He was the first person to suggest that it might take only a small percentage of a population to undergo a shift into greater coherence for the whole population to shift. Ken Keyes popularized this notion with the concept of the "hundredth monkey." More recently, Malcolm Gladwell wrote the *New York Times* bestseller *The Tipping Point*, in which he credibly demonstrates how shifts in the collective start with a few people. Once that number reaches a critical mass, Gladwell posits, the whole social system shifts all at once. By now, the notion has settled quite deeply into mainstream understanding. Evolutionary shifts require only a few key people to act as catalysts for the whole.

It is difficult to communicate in words quite what it feels like to be in Varadaiahpalem today. You need only see the looks in the children's eyes and the way people are with each other to appreciate what has happened there. The whole town has become like one family. People help each other, care for each other, pray for each other. Certainly, there are many, many outward and material changes, and we could list them here. The villagers have better living conditions now, but that is almost a by-product. For they are very quickly gaining something else, something rare to find anywhere in the world: happy people living and working together in a happy society.

I walked the streets of Varadaiahpalem and several other surrounding villages. Many people tell me their health has greatly improved since the university arrived. There are now mobile health units going to all the villages, but mostly it is attributed to healings at the large Oneness deeksha events. Alcohol consumption has diminished to less than 20 percent of its previous levels. I walked or drove past the liquor store dozens of times and never saw a single customer inside. Domestic violence is almost eliminated; the villagers I asked told me, through translators, that they had not heard of any incidents for months. There are no longer fights in the streets, leaving the police force of fifteen constables with much less to do. A government official told me, on strict condition of anonymity, that the cops are mostly playing cards these days.

The economy has boomed, and unemployment is down so low that anyone who wants to work can do so. This is due, in part, to the dasas having helped set up community projects, such as a local incense factory that offers employment—as well as a strong sense of vision—to hundreds of local women. Buffalo herds and goats have been given to local people to tend.

The local school is the greatest miracle. When I visited, I did not want to leave. It felt more like the kids were enjoying a magic show than going to school. Sitting cross-legged on the floor, the children threw their hands into the air to answer the teacher's questions. Although still relatively poor, the kids, with their bright eyes and infectious laughter, were captivating. When the class was done, many went to hug their teacher. Some children stay till six or seven at night for extra classes. In the 2005–2006 academic year, students from several grades achieved the highest ranks in the whole *mandal,* the local community of 64,000 people. The school, which used to only go to the American equivalent of eighth grade, now continues to twelfth grade and prepares pupils for university entrance.

The youth of the Hundred Village Project have been the most transformed. All have been invited to take the university's youth programs as guests. Several told me that their relationship with their parents has changed dramatically and that, for the first time, they have discovered vision and the possibility of a meaningful life.

All of this was very impressive in and of itself when I visited these villages. But what amazed me even more was what has started to happen for individual villagers in precipitating higher states of consciousness. Chengalvarayan and his wife, Lalitha, have lived in Varadaiahpalem for four years with their daughter, Devi Priya, and their son, Praveen Kumra. They arrived at about the same time as the dasas. A weaver by trade, Chengalvarayan sits at a loom all day, making handcrafted saris for which the area is famous. He does not read or write. The family lives together in one hut, about ten feet by fifteen feet. "I used to live lavishly, beyond my means," he told me. "I accumulated lots of debts in the neighborhood." Like most of the local men, this meant going on drinking sprees and then coming home drunk and hitting his wife and small children. Lalitha and both the children told me that they used to be very afraid of him.

Chengalvarayan attended one Oneness deeksha event a few months before our meeting. He was taken there by a family member. As he describes it, when the dasa put his hands on this simple weaver's head, there was an immediate silence;

all thought stopped. That absolute stillness has never left. Chengalvarayan was instantaneously thrown into an awakening out of the mind with a single Oneness deeksha, with absolutely no previous background or interest in anything spiritual at all. When you speak with him, this silence is palpable. His eyes are unwavering; his body, completely still and at peace. It is a depth of presence I had previously only seen in a few highly respected spiritual teachers and long-term Tibetan Buddhist practitioners.

A few doors down lives Subba Nagamma, one of the oldest inhabitants of the village. Her hut has three rooms, where she lives with one of her two sons, his wife, and their two children. They also make handwoven saris, right there in the hut. She was unable to walk a few years back but was healed by her first Oneness deeksha. She describes how things are now:

> There are no thoughts in the mind. There is constant internal joy. Because people might consider me insane if I were to laugh constantly, I hold it within myself. Even the members of my family cannot understand my joy. That is why I hide it. Otherwise, it is constant bliss for me. It is constant happiness. What little anger I had also has left me. Suffering has left me. Bhagavan has removed it all—my anger, my pain—completely. He has only given me bliss and happiness. We are people who work and earn for the day and survive. But that itself is now great satisfaction, fulfillment, and joy.

I met dozens of people like this in Varadaiahpalem. They had obviously undergone some kind of permanent shift toward deep inner stillness, causeless love, and joy. Every night, groups of dasas go into one of these 140 villages and conduct Oneness deeksha events. As you may recall, there are dasas who are able to read the state of the brain. According to these dasas' readings, between six and ten more villagers are Awakening into Oneness and becoming stable each night. Very often, this is happening on their first Oneness deeksha.

As you may remember, when Anandagiri first came to visit the villages just a few years ago, no one wanted his classes—they all wanted electricity and TVs. Now that these shifts are happening, the village is becoming much more prosperous. The dasas are helping to get everyone work, to get books and uniforms and cooked lunches for the schools. But these material improvements are not what most villagers ask for nowadays. They now ask for *mukti*, or liberation. "This has become the cry on everyone's lips," says Anandagiri. "Mukti, mukti, mukti. Give us mukti. They are all crazy for mukti!"

In the summer of 2006, the dasas estimated that more than seven hundred villagers had already passed through this shift into awakening, which we will explore in much greater depth in the next chapter. The vision for the Hundred Village Project is that if enough villagers can shift in this way, then the shift will happen for the community as a whole, allowing us to see awakening at a collective level. Who knows? By the time you finish reading this book, awakening may be the norm in Varadaiahpalem.

MIRACLES IN MEXICO

We discover more about how the Oneness Blessing can affect the collective from the stories of Alexis Shaffer. Her stories sound like they came straight out of *Ripley's Believe It or Not!* After her training to become a Oneness Blessing giver, Alexis was visiting Mexico from her home in Spain, when she was invited by friends to visit the small historic town of San Cristobal de las Casas, in the state of Chiapas. The Sunday she was there, she awoke with a clear vision: that day, she would give the Blessing to a thousand people. She had no idea how this might happen. After walking around the town for a while, she came upon a square in front of a church. At the center of the square stood a simple cross on a platform with some steps leading up to it. She sat down there and started giving Blessings. She offered virtually no explanation except that this was a "blessing from God." By evening, a crowd had formed. When she went back the next day, the crowd had grown. The police showed up and informed her she would need permission to be there. She was sent off to the municipal hall to get an official paper. One thing led to another, and by the time she finally got permission from the right official, she had given the Oneness Blessing to the entire office staff.

She returned to the square, where over the following days, she gave the Oneness Blessing to several thousand people. As the crowd grew, so did the number of police supervising these unusual events. Finally, one of the police asked Alexis, "Why don't you come to the police station to give us all the Blessing there? There are over four hundred policemen." She went along the next day. And so began Alexis's extraordinary journey giving Blessings to every kind of Mexican man and woman in uniform. From the police station, she moved to the mayor's municipal palace, where she gave Blessings to the mayor and the entire municipal staff—more than a thousand people. From there, she had another vision: to move on to the military. She promptly made an appointment to see the local general. She explained that she had already given the Oneness Blessing to everyone in town, including the mayor. "Okay," said the general. "You've already done this with all my friends, so let's see what it is all about. What do I have to do?"

"Just sit down, close your eyes, take a deep breath, relax, and move into your heart," replied Alexis. "Imagine yourself like a baby general, all curled up, resting in a corner of your heart." As you can perhaps imagine, this was not the usual military language to which the general was accustomed. Just as she was going to put her hands on the general's head, she noticed the general grasping the sides of the chair in a death grip, his muscles bulging. Alexis tapped him on the knee. "Excuse me, Mr. General, but you don't look very relaxed." He opened his eyes, noticed what he was doing, and they both burst out laughing. The general loved his Blessing, and Alexis went on to give Blessings to all his men.

You think I'm making all this up, don't you? The resources section at the end of the book will direct you to Alexis's website, where you can read hundreds of these stories, see pictures, and read testimonials and letters.

When Alexis arrived in Cancun, there was no messing around. She went straight to the most senior general she could find there. She told him about the events in Chiapas, which created enough trust in him that he was ready to try the Oneness Blessing himself. He felt relief from a pain that had been bothering him for more than a year. He then gave her a test group of a hundred men. This group had been practicing a twenty-one-gun salute and just couldn't get it right. Alexis gave them all the Oneness Blessing. The next day, they all shot together at the same time. The general was so impressed that he gave her his entire battalion of more than seven hundred men for a week.

"Please harmonize them," he asked Alexis. "Give them peace and tranquility." Right afterward, the men went away for a month of training. It was the first time in military history that 750 men returned from a month of training without one injury, conflict, or problem.

Alexis has gone on to work with the Federal Commission of Electricity, the convention of the tourism industry, firemen, security personnel, more than sixteen thousand taxi drivers—the list goes on and on. She has found again and again that by working with a few people out of a larger organization, the entire group dynamic shifts into more harmony and cooperation—into Oneness.

ONENESS BLESSINGS IN THE CHURCH

Churches all over the world have been transformed by the power of the Oneness Blessing. In Christian communities, it has been called the Oneness Prayer; in mosques, it is often given by placing the Koran on the head; and in Buddhist communities, it can be called the Oneness Meditation. In Sweden, Marie Ryd has been offering the Oneness Blessing for more than a year in one of Stockholm's largest churches, at the invitation of the priests. All over the United States, the Oneness Blessing has been integrated into the weekly activities of Unity churches, from Seattle to Miami. But nowhere has the impact on church communities been as strong as in East Africa. In the summer of 2005, five bishops traveled to the Oneness University and underwent a twenty-one-day Oneness Process. Now they are giving Blessings in all their services throughout Tanzania, Uganda, Kenya, Zimbabwe, Congo, and South Africa. More than 150,000 people have received the Oneness Blessing in these services, where often many thousands will receive the Blessing at the same time.

Bishop Werema is the leader of the Enaboishu Baptist Church in Tanzania. He has seen a huge shift in his congregation:

When they receive the Oneness Blessing, the people get a whole new attitude; they become like a new person. Sometimes it takes just a few hours, or a few days or a week. They no longer differentiate "this person I like, this person I don't like." They see everyone as their brother

or sister; they want to help each other. They become one, like the same
body, like the same person. When you see another person, you are see-
ing yourself. You'd like to stay together always. The Lord Jesus Christ
would like us to love each other, to have peace, to have joy, and this is
what we get with the Oneness Blessing. So I feel it is the same thing
as Jesus's teaching.

Shosin Sugasawa is the chief priest of the Chouon temple in Tochigi Prefecture in Japan. He educates monks in the ancient teachings of Shingon esoteric Buddhism. He gives Oneness deeksha, as it is known in Japan, to everyone he teaches now, both Zen monks and laypeople. When he conducts a special ceremony for people to be united with Dainichi Nyorai, the most important deity in Shingon, he reports that now he simply gives intentional deeksha, and people feel divine presence immediately. "Many people are stuck in trying to get enlightenment," he says. "But if you can just be in the energy of Oneness deeksha, you are naturally in higher intelligence, higher consciousness in divine presence. The process of enlightenment just starts automatically. Oneness deeksha is far beyond penance or ascetic practices."

ONENESS BLESSINGS IN PRISON

James Beard has been working in the Los Angeles County jail system since 1979. He primarily works with inmates who are in for domestic violence, drugs, and gang activity. Instead of being locked up in a prison cell, these men come to him in a classroom setting for eight hours a day and then go to sleep in a dormitory. He has a mandate from the county to offer programs that will raise their level of consciousness through understanding themselves, through any kind of spiritual experience, and to develop an internal focus of self-control. Within these existing programs, he started to invite Oneness Blessing givers into the prison in 2005. Soon after, he became a Blessing giver himself. He now offers Blessings once a week to all the inmates in his programs.

The first thing he noticed after introducing the Oneness Blessing was that whatever else he was teaching was absorbed faster:

They now get really deep information at a faster rate and at a deeper level. For example, I might try to explain to them that your life moves toward your intention. Previously, it would take me about a week or so to get them to understand what that means. Now that I give them Oneness Blessings, they get it almost instantly.

He finds that by giving the Oneness Blessing just once a week, the atmosphere of the facility has changed a great deal. The inmates and the other guards have all commented that it feels lighter, that a heaviness has lifted.

One of the greatest challenges Beard has had to face in working in the prison system is the strict segregation of races:

Blacks do not associate with Hispanics; Hispanics do not associate with whites. In the county jail system, different ethnic groups never mingle together. Since the Oneness Blessing, though, they are drinking out of each other's cups at meals. This is totally outside the page of anything else in the country. Now they have a deep spiritual knowledge of each other.

Beard remembers one particular young African American man to whom he gave the Oneness Blessing in the beginning. He was a very big, powerful man who was in for beating up his girlfriend and for gang-related activity. The morning after the first Blessing, he was waiting. "I had a dream yesterday," he said. "After you told me to lie down after the Blessing, I dreamt that I was in my mother's womb, that I was an embryo. Then I felt myself grow into a baby, still inside my mother's stomach. Then I felt myself being born. Once I came out, all of a sudden everything changed, and I became myself looking at myself being born. But that's not all. This morning I received a call, and my new baby son was born last night."

"After that," Beard reports, "there was a glow in that young man's eyes. His speech became deliberate; he would look you in the eyes. Whenever he would ask a question, the question had to do with his own individual growth and development. It was never about anybody else."

Daveed Constantine has been working for the last three years as a volunteer with violent inmates at San Quentin. Due to restrictions on touching the prisoners as a volunteer, he gives Oneness Blessings through the eyes or just through intention. He, too, says that before the Blessing, the men were very disconnected. "They might have seen each other for years, but they didn't establish any conscious relationship." He also reported an initial separation between ethnic groups. "Sometimes they had no connection whatsoever. To just be together, to start connecting together and doing processes together, built a group identity. That has kept on growing. They are kinder to each other; they help each other. It has become a kind of a fellowship inside there now. There is a sense of community and brotherhood."

According to the Bureau of Justice Statistics, in mid-2005, there were 2,186,230 people imprisoned in the United States. This works out to 488 per 100,000 citizens, making America the country with the highest percentage of its population behind bars in the world. More than half of those imprisoned are in for nonviolent crimes. So when I had the opportunity to interview Bhagavan for this book, I asked what his message to these millions of prisoners would be, if he had a chance to address them:

> My feeling about people in prison is that if they were not in prison, we would be the ones in prison. A certain balance is being maintained in society. They have committed some crimes, and they are in prison. And had they not committed those crimes, we would be the ones who would have committed them. That's why I have special love for these people. It is our duty to help them out, and hence I give special deeksha powers to those who work in jails.

INDIGENOUS PEOPLE

In the fall of 2005, Rani Kumra shared the Oneness Blessing at an annual gathering of native elders from all over the world, and invited them as her guests to come to India for a special twenty-one-day Oneness Process. Thirteen were able to make the journey. The process was quite different for these people. They already share a common and ancient recognition for the oneness of all things and for the respect of elders and an understanding for the earth's natural cycles. Although the language and the countries were different, the underlying energy was the same. This allowed them to quickly feel comfortable and to connect with each other and with Bhagavan, Amma, and the dasas. Bhagavan holds a special place in his heart for indigenous people. When he met with them, he told them they would be pivotal in helping humanity to heal.

Christine Bullock is a Maori grandmother. She facilitates cross-cultural exchange programs among indigenous peoples all over the world:

Once you go through the Oneness Process, you just accept who you are. You come back into that space of trust, innocence of knowing, and universal belonging. I think everybody in the world should have that three weeks of just sitting and finding that sense of self again. It's extraordinary; it's beyond words. The generosity of sharing, not just within their own culture, but with all of us, was amazing.

Tom Ross is a Dakota elder who served on the Indigenous Peoples Working Group at the United Nations and works in treatment centers for alcohol and gambling addictions:

My experience at the Oneness University was a really healing process for me. I came back considerably healthier than when I left. People noticed. I was going to participate in a study for my heart condition, but after I returned, I no longer fit the criteria. In terms of energy, I now have what I need to get out and do the work I do. And I experienced a deeper connection to the spiritual traditions of the Dakota.

Serene Thin Elk, a little sister of the Dakota and master of the sacred flute, is a graduate student in expressive arts therapy. She shares a common wound with all native peoples: an experience of displacement. Like all indigenous people, she carries the collective pain that has been inflicted on her people for generations. "I thought about that a lot when I was there. Nothing was really said about it, but you could feel it. I could feel it in myself, and I could see it in other people. It was like a lot of the things that we carried were just lifted."

Although the Maori of New Zealand have been quite fortunate compared with other groups colonized by Western people, they also have experienced cultural disruption that has contributed to substance abuse and domestic violence. Christine is also the chairwoman of Te Kopere O Rachina, a Maori healing and teaching center:

Prior to going to India, I carried resentment in my heart for what has been done to all of us. When you work with the native people and see how they have suffered, it sits very heavy with you. Since we've been to India, we understand things better. We're not taking it onboard personally. We're just acknowledging it, doing the little prayers to help our people. But we're not carrying it. I think that's one thing that the Oneness Blessing has shown us—that oppression exists and will continue to be in the world, but you don't have to carry it in your heart. You can acknowledge it but not feed it.

Most native peoples from all over the world share a respect and reverence for elders, and they found this echoed in southern India. Christine continues:

The elders are the most beloved and treasured part of our culture because they hold the knowledge; they hold the energy. Without them, we're lost. Many of us actually found a grandfather and grandmother in Bhagavan and Amma. To find people who could be that for so many different cultures at once was extraordinary.

The entire group, in their native dress, had the opportunity to meet with Bhagavan both as a group and individually. Serene remembers:

It took just one time sitting with him as a group, speaking with him and sharing our stories, for us to feel immense love. It was one of the most amazing things that has ever happened to me. Bhagavan shared

a little bit about the role he felt indigenous people would play in help-
ing raise consciousness—how we had the ability to go back into our
communities and not only heal our people and the land, but also heal
some of the relationships that we have with society as a whole.

After three weeks, they were ready to return home and share their renewed
sense of hope and vision. They had a gift that they could bring back to their
people. Serene first shared the Oneness Blessing with her family, who were
open, and some had profound experiences. Her brother, who has struggled
with addiction for ten years, said that he felt hope in a way that he had never
felt in his entire life. "I think it's really the beginning of something powerful,"
says Serene. "Not only for our family but also for our tribe. It will emanate
from there."

During a ceremony in India, Serene had a vision that echoed Bhagavan's
vision for the native people of the world:

I felt the presence of all our ancestors, and it was really very powerful.
My eyes were closed the whole time, but I was seeing all these things, and
I felt someone come behind me and start caressing my head. The feeling
and the message I got was, "It's gonna be okay." I felt this surge of hope,
which was actually beyond hope. I knew that a great healing was going
to take place. I knew that we were all a part of an intricate process, one
that will allow all of us to see that great healing come to be.

CHAPTER ELEVEN

THE ONENESS BLESSING AND HIGHER STATES OF CONSCIOUSNESS

T hus far, we've mainly discussed the effects of the Oneness Blessing on the individual: you feel healthier; your relationships improve; you make more money; you make a greater contribution to the world around you. According to Bhagavan and the dasas, however, the ultimate potential of the Oneness Blessing is much more than this. The Blessing can precipitate a shift toward a completely different state of consciousness, where the sense of "me" as a separate entity dissolves. What remains is a simple and direct realization of Oneness, unclouded by the conceptual mind. The Oneness Blessing has been able to catalyze this shift for thousands of people, both in India and in the rest of the world. This is something so profoundly simple and glorious that it defies logical description. Oneness is the heart's deepest longing, the song of the ages.

Before we can really explore and appreciate the significance of what the Oneness Blessing offers in this way, however, we need to address a number of misunderstandings that have spawned most of the criticism of this phenomenon in recent years, particularly on the Internet. In the first chapter of this book, I promised to report not only on the good news but also on the most common criticisms.

The first criticism concerns what the celebrated Tibetan Buddhist teacher Lama Surya Das calls "premature immaculation." By this, he means that someone has a peak spiritual experience and then clings to the memory of that experience in the mind, persuading themselves, and anyone else who will listen, that they have reached the pinnacles of enlightenment. Some critics feel that the Oneness movement has spawned one of the greatest outbreaks of premature immaculation in living memory. After the first twenty-one-day courses started, the overall focus of deeksha givers (as they were then known in the West) was on peak experiences: either craving for them or repeating stories about them in the way that a fisherman goes on and on boasting about the size of his catch . . . several years ago. Little weight was given to human values like modesty, integrity, and honesty. Many were traveling the world, claiming to be in a "permanent state of enlightenment." This obsession with "me" and "my enlightenment," the need to repeat stories from the past, and the claims of ultimate states where evolution (and honest self-reflection) had ceased caused many at that time to dismiss all this as just another backwater of the spiritualized ego.

When we were first invited to India to visit Bhagavan, my wife, Chameli, and I both had serious reservations, largely because of these kinds of claims. We had met many of the claimants, and their claims just did not ring true. The book I had just finished researching and writing was a fairly thorough examination of this kind of mythology—of "enlightenment" as a point of final arrival. On my way to Oneness University, I felt like Michael Moore on his way to the Republican National Convention. But something deeper than thinking or logic was pulling at us to go, and so we went anyway.

Our socks were thoroughly blown off.

When I was asked to write the Oneness book, I wondered how I could present these self-professed claims of sainthood with a straight face. But I liked everything else so much, I was willing to give it a try.

The word "enlightenment" has been used so widely that it does not have one, fixed meaning. Those who use the word agree neither on one state to which it refers nor on who is supposed to be enlightened and who is not. Bhagavan and the dasas in India have used the word in an unusual way: to refer to a specific threshold of neurological functioning. They claim that when the parietal-lobe activity comes to below 25 on the right side and 30 on the left (using their own system of intuitive measurement; this is not in microvolts) and when there is a differential of at least 20 of the left frontal lobe over the right, the brain has been healed. At this point, it undergoes a shift back into its natural state of functioning, and the trance of separation is lifted. They also claim that once the brain comes into such balance, it will usually stay that way—rather like getting over an illness. As you may remember, a number of dasas have the capacity to read the state of anyone's brain, anywhere in the world, similar to a medical intuitive or a dowser. It is claimed that these dasas can read the level of activity in the parietal lobes, the frontal lobes, and other parts of the brain. And hence they can determine how much that person's brain is supportive of awakened consciousness.

Assuming that the people I had met who claimed permanent enlightenment were the same ones who had passed this threshold, I overcame my scruples, made a list of about twenty such "Oneness celebrities" to interview for this book, and took the list to Pragyanand, our dasa, for confirmation. He glanced down the list in a perfunctory sort of a way. "Nope, nope, not even close, nope, far away, nope, nope." Now, here was a strange situation. This was an organization with a reputation for giving enlightenment, and yet all the people claiming to be enlightened did not pass the test! I asked him if there was *anyone* who fitted the brain-dowsing dasas' criteria. He told me I would have to ask Bhagavan.

Bhagavan confirmed that I had the wrong list. All those big-fish stories were just that: stories about peak experiences in the past. He told me that at that time there were more than a hundred Westerners whose brains had passed this threshold, not to mention all the 170 dasas and several hundred Indians, but they were not the same people making all the noise about it. That was December 2005. At the time this book goes to press, there are now several hundred Westerners and several thousand Indians, and by the time you read this, it will certainly be many more. I pressed him for names, and he gave me half a dozen.

Armed with this list of names, I returned to the United States to begin researching this book. I have interviewed all the people whose names he gave me—many were already our friends—as well as dozens of others whose names I was given later. We will hear more from them later. Although they are outwardly as different from each other as one can imagine, this excerpt from an interview is very typical:

Arjuna: When I was in India, Bhagavan told me that your parietal-lobe activity had gone below a certain threshold that he would describe as enlightened. According to him, that's an irreversible sort of a thing. So what does that mean to you? What does the word "enlightenment" mean to you? How do you relate to it?

Interviewee: [bursts out laughing for about thirty seconds] *Oh, that's sweet. I don't know how to answer that. I feel fine. I feel great. I really don't think about enlightenment very much at all. I don't experience anything strange or unusual. I wouldn't really say I have a state to talk about. I am living my life.*

She changed the subject to something more interesting. She was really not very interested in talking about herself at all.

Another one on the list had just returned home after being away for many months of traveling. He told me his house was in need of repair:

There is a leak here in the gutters, the door needs fixing, and the deck needs staining. So these days, I am the handyman. I get up, and my day is about the nails and the paint. I don't think about my state or anything spiritual. I am doing what I am doing, and it is all very simple.

When I returned to India for the second time, and we did the interviews for this book, I asked Bhagavan about the many claims being made for "permanent enlightenment." He responded:

These people seem to have their own idea of enlightenment, and therefore declare themselves to be enlightened. Maybe we are also responsible for that! There are some people who are actually enlightened, who know clearly that they are enlightened. We have checked and found it to be true. There are also people who have become enlightened but are not aware that they are enlightened, some of whom we have had to educate. And then they became clear.

The Indian sage Yogananda was once at a press conference where a journalist asked him, "Are you enlightened?" Yogananda was silent for some time, but the journalist persisted. Finally, he answered like this: "If someone says, 'I am enlightened,' they are probably not enlightened. If someone says, 'I am not enlightened,' they are probably not enlightened." Then Yogananda was silent. Why? Because if enlightenment means anything at all, it means the complete dissolution of interest in a separate "me." The words "I" and "enlightenment" do not belong together in the same sentence.

Another criticism that has been directed at this movement might be described as "broken promises." Some people who took the early courses in 2004 feel that they were promised "permanent enlightenment in twenty-one days." Some say they were disappointed. They were told they had entered a state of permanent enlightenment, but when they got home, the state seemed to dissipate.

How could an organization be genuinely catalyzing awakening in so many people while also developing a reputation for being a scam? Was it all too good to be true? Were followers of other paths jealous and giving it a bad rap on the Web? Was all this just a lot of buzz, created by overly enthusiastic followers, or was there more to it? What did Bhagavan mean by "Maybe we are also responsible for that"?

On my second visit to India, a good part of the interviews I conducted with Bhagavan and the dasas were about this topic. They offered multiple layers of clarification. Their understanding of the nature of states of consciousness is both subtle and multidimensional, like stepping into a quantum universe. We could fill volumes exploring these topics, but they can also be distilled down to seven essential points.

1. Experience, More Than Teachings

Ever since the twenty-one-day Oneness Process began, very little emphasis has been placed on teachings or explanation. As Anandagiri explained to me:

There have been so many teachings throughout history, so many books written. But they have not made so much difference. Our work here is to change the brain, and that will change the way you experience yourself and everything else. Then you can come to your own conclusions; you can create your own teachings.

So the whole emphasis of the Oneness Process is on clearing old traumas from the nervous system, developing a deep familiarity with silence, facing oneself in a profound way, and having direct realization of the divine. At some point, something may be said loosely about enlightenment, without much explanation. This is one factor that has contributed to both exaggerated claims and to the letdown some feel: people grab on to a word and give it their own meaning.

2. Cultural Differences in the Use of Language

Bhagavan and Amma have never been outside India. In fact, they have never traveled outside the states of Andhra Pradesh and Tamil Nadu in the south. The same is true for most of the dasas: only a handful have been outside India, and then only for short periods of time. Until 2004, the dasas had guided hundreds of thousands of Indians in courses—and fewer than two hundred Westerners. Since then, many more Westerners have come, and it has taken some time for the cultural differences to be bridged. There are huge differences between the cultures of southern India and the West, particularly the way they use language. In the West, a great importance is placed on accuracy, on "keeping one's word." If you say something and then do another or something else happens, you may be seen as untrustworthy.

The same importance that is given to accuracy in the West is given to "auspicious intent" in India, particularly in the south. Words are used to inspire a good and relaxed feeling of optimism, to set everyone's focus on the best-case scenario. They are not taken as literally as they are in the West. Hence, explained Radhakrishna, the leader of the Oneness Process for Americans, when Bhagavan declared in early courses that everyone would become "enlightened," it was meant more to inspire confidence. It was a statement that would set the right tone for the course, that would yield the best results. "Sometimes when that is told, when it is taken in the right sense, it has a great impact on people. When it is not taken in that sense, the whole essence is lost. It all depends on how the person is receiving that input." I met many Indians who had also participated in the courses at the Oneness University. They had heard the same kinds of statements about enlightenment, but for them, it was never a contractual promise. So no one was disappointed. It was interpreted more as a blessing on their sacred voyage.

3. Psychological Differences Between the Indian and Western Minds

When the first courses were offered to Western visitors, the experiences were extraordinary. Even those who later complained about broken promises spoke to me about having felt totally one with God, about the mind stopping completely for long periods, about the absolute dissolution of any sense of separation. For the dasas, used to working with Indian participants at that time, it was unimaginable that such a state could be lost. It seems that the Western psyche can dissolve into enlightened states without much problem, but the sense of "me" enthusiastically bounces back with relative ease. You can get the horse to the water, it will take a good drink, and then it will gallop off again in search of other distractions. For the Indian psyche, on the other hand, it may be relatively difficult to get the horse to the water, but once you do, it quickly drowns and is not seen again. Not only is the psyche different, but so is the culture into which Western visitors are returning. India has been steeped in mukti for thousands of years; the West, on the other hand, glorifies the sense of a "me" and seeks to reinforce it at every turn. So a return to a village in Tamil Nadu will present much less challenge than a return to New York City.

4. The Dissolving of "Me"

Today, a much greater distinction is made at the Oneness University between an enlightened state and the irreversible dissolving of the sense of a separate self. One is an experience—among many others—of an entity called "me." The other is the ceasing to reference that "me" altogether. The claims made by early graduates pertained to memories of enlightened states, but their sense of "I" was still very much intact. It was that "I" who was now making claims of being enlightened. Bhagavan explains:

> From our point of view, if somebody gets the enlightened state, there's every possibility of this becoming enlightenment. So the moment he gets the enlightened state, we will say, "Yes, you have made it." But

the state itself is only temporary in nature. It may go away. Because we said, "You have made it," they think that they are permanently enlightened. This is a never-ending process; it will eventually result in enlightenment. Sometimes the enlightened state does not lead to enlightenment at all.

5. Seven Billion Kinds of Enlightenment

The claims that have been made for "full enlightenment" or "permanent enlightenment" presuppose that enlightenment is one, fixed condition, the same for everyone. "To say 'you made it' can be misleading," says Radhakrishna, "because it sounds like it is the same for everybody. But actually, the flowering will be different in every flower. You can't compare the blossoming of a rose and a daffodil. They have different colors and different smells, different everything." In fact, says Bhagavan, there are as many varieties of enlightenment as there are people on the planet. One distinction he makes has to do with which chakra is more activated. He recognizes twenty-one *chakras,* or energy centers: seven in the body (in the same locations as the ductless glands), seven above the body, and seven below. When the heart chakra is activated, for example, enlightenment is experienced as unconditional love. Bhagavan calls this Christian enlightenment. Similarly, when the *vishutti chakra* in the throat is activated, there is great peace, which he calls Muslim enlightenment. Enlightenment in the third eye is experienced as emptiness, which he calls Buddhist enlightenment. Finally, when the crown chakra is activated, it is experienced as oneness with everything, which he calls Hindu enlightenment.

6. An Endless Journey

While the early claims for a state of "permanent enlightenment" sounded like an arrival, Bhagavan speaks of the crossing of the threshold in the brain as the beginning of an endless process:

Enlightenment is the first step. It is the beginning of the real journey. First you get an enlightened state, a peak experience, which has to result in enlightenment sooner or later. After that, it is a never-ending process.

The process ultimately stops only when you merge into light. Until then, it goes on and on. It will go on while you are on this planet. After you've left the planet, it still continues. There is no end to it.

He compares the mind to a boxing match, where different personalities are always in conflict with one another. Before any kind of an awakening, you feel like you are inside the ring, getting punched continually, from every side. When the brain passes through the thresholds mentioned above, you step out of the ring. The conflict continues, but you now know that it is not happening to you. As the brain continues to shift, the process deepens, and even the fighting can become less frequent. Then one day, the boxers finally stop fighting, sit down together, and have tea. Then the ring itself disappears, and there is absolute stillness.

7. Waves in an Ocean

Although awakening may appear to be an individual phenomenon, happening to him over there and to her over here, the shift that the Oneness Blessing is precipitating is actually collective. As the awakening deepens, there is less and less interest in "me." There comes the recognition that these are not *my* thoughts—they are all part of the collective mind; they belong to all of humanity. Pain is *our* pain; resistance is *our* resistance. And, too, the liberation that the heart calls for is *our* liberation. There cannot be full liberation in any one mind until there is liberation in the collective, because just below the surface appearance, they are one and the same. For a wave in the ocean to become warmer, the whole ocean must become warmer; they are the same. One little wave might aspire to become tropically cozy, but if it is dancing in the middle of the Atlantic in December, it's not going to happen. None of us can drift very far from the collective consciousness in which we dance, of which we are made. In this realization, aspirations for and claims of enlightenment dissipate into service to all sentient beings, to the Oneness—for that is what we all really are. The quantum shift of which we are all a part, and of which the Oneness Blessing is a catalyst, is one that includes and carries all of us as one.

• • •

All the above points are relevant mainly to the past. They are useful to know if you have Googled this phenomenon on the Web or heard criticisms or met people claiming to be more enlightened than Buddha, or even if you participated in a course a few years back and have been tempted to make such claims yourself. Most of these misunderstandings have now been cleared up. At a recent conference of more than a thousand people in Sweden, one participant asked a question about promises of enlightenment. Acharya Anandagiri simply answered, "If we gave you that impression, it was a mistake, and we apologize." That was it; everyone took a breath, and things moved on. Partly to distance themselves from the confusion that the word can create, Bhagavan and the dasas are using the word "enlightenment" less and less, and talk more about "awakening" and "oneness." So this is the language we will use here for the brain that has been healed of the hallucination of separation: Awakening into Oneness. And finally, many of those who made grand claims in the past have climbed down from the roof and joined the party with the rest of humanity, so these exaggerated claims are becoming a thing of the past.

THE PERFUME OF ONENESS

During the process of writing this book, I interviewed dozens of people whose brains have passed through the thresholds Bhagavan describes as necessary to support Awakening into Oneness. They come from a variety of backgrounds. Some are illiterate villagers in India, who needed a translator to tell me their story. Some are celebrities, whose names you surely know. Some are spiritual writers or teachers, veterans of spiritual life. And just as many are completely new to all this: the shift in the brain came after a few Oneness Blessings, before which they had never read a single spiritual book. Some are extremely wealthy businesspeople; some are monks with no possessions at all. Some are the dasas close to Bhagavan. Some had received Blessings a few times, but had no affiliation at all to the organization. The only thing these people have in common is that they have nothing whatsoever in common. If we brought them together at a party with an equal number of "regular" people, you would have a hard time figuring out who was who.

Awakening into Oneness is more of a subtle perfume than a blazing neon sign. It is discreet. After a while, you get to recognize its fragrance. The majority of the people who have passed over this threshold do not talk about it. If pressed, they will acknowledge that things are different now, but you have to pry it out of them. The awakened heart is not a big dog jumping on you and enthusiastically licking your face. In respect for that natural modesty most of them share, I have omitted names in the quotes that follow. This seems appropriate in light of the fact that most of these people now feel more oceanic than like isolated waves.

The subjective experiences associated with Awakening into Oneness may, in fact, precede the shifts in the brain, they may accompany those shifts, or they may start to manifest sometime later. The shifts in the brain provide the necessary neurology to support awakening in an effortless and spontaneous way. It is certainly possible to have strong and sustained glimpses before the brain has shifted, just as it is still possible to experience separation in snapshots *after* the brain has shifted. "The awakening happened for me in 1999," said one of those I interviewed. "When Bhagavan told me that the lobes had now shifted, he explained that it was simply that the brain had now caught up with my subjective experience." Others reported the opposite: "It has only been since I got home and have been around other people that I see the contrast. I feel more normal than I ever have before in my life. When I listen to how other people are experiencing reality, then I see it. I realize that they are getting caught up in things that I can no longer imagine getting caught up in."

Following are some of the subjective indicators of Awakening into Oneness. Some of those interviewed displayed some of these indicators much more than others, but all these qualities were present to some degree in everyone I spoke with. It is important, in reading this, to understand that these qualities are the spontaneous result of shifts in the brain. They are not recipes for awakening. Trying to imitate these qualities if they are not arising spontaneously could actually delay awakening rather than propel it.

There Is Nobody Here

Although life goes on in the usual way and it is still possible to use words like "I" and "me" when needed, the sense of a fixed entity to which those words point has dissolved. It's not that the "ego" or the "I" has been destroyed; rather, it becomes clear that nothing like that has ever existed at all. It was a hallucination. Thoughts come and go on their own—they are happening, but there is clearly no thinker and no one and nothing to control them. Talking about oneself becomes uninteresting. It is all stories about someone who does not exist.

This includes the story of "my enlightenment." There are really three relationships one can have with the concept of enlightenment. One would be, "Look at me. I have made it!" The second would be, "I have not made it, and I am waiting to make it." And the third would be, "Not applicable." The whole question simply no longer makes any sense. All the people I interviewed who were reputed to have passed through this shift in the brain were in category three. The preoccupation with enlightenment, either as an attainment or as a goal, has been replaced with a generosity of spirit, a willingness to serve and be used. One interviewee told me:

> There was the moment where I felt like the whole galaxy was inside, and it was just a little breeze. Then there was just nothing. It was really nothing, and that was so liberating. That's beauty. I had had the giggles all day. But then the laughter became a roar. It was so funny to see how, all our lives, we have been seeking, seeking something that doesn't exist. That was the cosmic joke, you know, the sacred game. I thought it was really funny. I don't know what enlightenment is or how much shutting down of the brain it takes. All I know is that for me, there was a dramatic difference in my view of the world before and my view of the world now. It's as if I had taken a drug—that's how strong.

Pure Experiencing

When sounds are heard without any interpretation and things are seen without any commentary, everything becomes fascinating; even small things become a source of joy:

I went outside; I saw a different world. The butterflies—I could follow them, as though they were flying in slow motion. Every sound was beautiful, even a door slamming. Sometimes I felt them inside my body. When somebody was whispering, it felt like it was right here, although they were way across the room. A dog kept coming up to me and wanting to play. I sat down on the grass. The dog was looking at me; the eyes were intense on me. I realized I had never really experienced a dog before.

Things become very simple. Like for the man who came home to his house in need of repair, life becomes just about nails and paint, whatever is before you, without the need to give it special meaning. In this simplicity, even the smallest things become a source of great joy: eating a piece of toast, hearing some music, watching the sun go down.

It's not like what I thought bliss would be. It is much subtler and much deeper, much less eventful, and yet there is great, great contentment inside of it. I don't know. So many things are really, really different from before, and yet words often put out something that it's not. It's not like high and always happy, the sun is shining all day long. It is subtler, much deeper; there is more stillness.

Things are experienced without any continuity: each moment is felt as unique and disconnected from any other moment. It becomes clear that the sense of continuity was only created in the mind.

An End of Personal Suffering

Although we still live in a world that has plenty of pain, and although the heart is still open in compassion to feel that pain, the sense of personal *suffering* is gone. We realize that suffering is to feel pain while trapped inside a soap opera. This was most beautifully illustrated by one of the people I spoke with who had grown up in New Orleans. Just a few weeks after his brain awoke into Oneness, he returned to New Orleans, a few months after the tragic hurricane that killed so many people. He called me on his cell phone:

I'm back in New Orleans where I grew up. When I first got here, I just drove all day, in the neighborhoods where I used to live. The Ninth Ward, where I grew up, is just gone. There are boats on top of houses. I lost five or six of my childhood friends. There are other people I knew who had a lot of money who are living in trailers now. But with all the woe that I see here right now, I'm able to stay on top of it and not get dragged down with it. It is amazing. I don't get upset with anything now. Nothing's gotten through to really bother me yet since the shift. Things come in, and they're there, but I just look at them and there's no attachment to it.

He was fully feeling the tragedy of what had occurred, yet it did not hook him. Many people speak in this way—of a mysterious absence of personal suffering. It's not that suffering is being avoided, but rather that there is no resistance to it. There is no longer any internal conflict. The end of suffering is the fruit of unconditional acceptance, rather than of chasing pleasure and avoiding pain.

Emotions still arise, like anger, jealousy, and sadness, but they pass very quickly. What might have lingered for hours, days, or weeks before is gone in a few minutes:

Emotions are like weather passing through. When they happen, I feel them so much deeper. There's no holding back. I think that might be the biggest difference of all. If I'm angry, I'm angry with every cell of my body. I'm not suppressing anything. And then it's over. And then this stillness and peace and joy come back rapidly.

Stillness

While thoughts and feelings continue, they are all discovered to be occurring in an ocean of stillness, just one flight down from the usual activity of the mind:

In India, I felt a sense of real stillness inside of me, complete stillness. Sometimes I would lie for five or six hours without moving even

once—not because I had to, but because my body was in that still-
ness. That is the place that I experience again and again, now that I
am home. It is a place that is absolutely still. Everything else happens
around it, and nothing changes on the outside. But something on the
inside is completely different.

The same activity of mind continues for almost everyone, but most reported that it now seems like someone else's mind, as though it were being
watched on a television. It becomes absurd.

I can feel the thoughts and how they are flowing. Before, I used to
be struggling with thoughts, trying to change the thoughts to some-
thing else. But now I can see the thoughts flowing away, without
any struggle, without trying to change the perception or trying to
change the thoughts themselves. Before, I used to struggle to change
the thoughts to fit whatever framework I had designed for my-
self. Now there is no framework; there is no person to change the
thoughts. The thoughts are just there flowing, flowing in nothing.
There is no container.

Many reported a humorous relationship to the personality, which now appears not as linear and cohesive but as fragmented and entirely on loan:

I hear myself say or do something, and I hear my mother or father,
or even a character from a TV cartoon when I was a child. Then a
few minutes or an hour later, I hear something completely different
coming from my mouth. None of it is really me. They are all person-
alities. They float in, and they float out. Sometimes no personality
is there at all.

Many also report that inner conflict dissipates after some time and eventually goes away entirely. Indecision and things that used to be troublesome
cease to cause any problem.

Trust

In the absence of inner conflict, one knows what to do quite naturally, without having to think about it. Our arduous mental processes are replaced by trust in, and surrender to, something invisible and universal. Many of those who have Awakened into Oneness through the Oneness Blessing feel an intense devotion to the divine will guiding them. They take their hands off the steering wheel and know that it is all unfolding perfectly. Earlier, I mentioned that these are all kinds of people. Here is a well-known rock musician whose brain has passed the threshold of awakening:

We don't see God everywhere only because we don't love ourselves enough. Now a lot of people are waking up and starting to feel that's not a cool way to live. Finally, we're starting to realize, "Hey, this is not working." You know? We're opening our eyes. We're starting to see God in a lot of things, in our daily basic experiences. Because God was always there. We just couldn't see Him, because nobody took solace and nobody let us know that God is everything. Everything is sacred. Brushing my teeth— everything can be a spiritual and sacred act. Nobody told us that.

Relationships Fall into Place

Perhaps the most universal and reliable indication of this shift into Oneness is a sense of intimacy with everything and everyone. It becomes virtually impossible to hold grudges; everyone feels like an ally. Even when people are acting against you, it is easy to see the unmet hurts in them that provoke them to behave that way. So forgiveness becomes a spontaneous and effortless result of that seeing. One woman I spoke with talks about her relationship with her partner—they used to fight much more before:

I feel so much more love for him and actual affection. I feel so much deeper when he touches me. Feeling his skin with my cheek, when I put my cheek into his hands, I'm experiencing things more fully. I guess I could say I'm experiencing things for the first time. I thought I could experience before, but it was nothing compared with how I now experience just talking to him, experiencing him. I can see when he's sad. I can see it so much more fully. I can see when his eyes are sad. I see his cheeks falling. I can see it so clearly. Any little shift in emotion is very apparent to me. You know, I melt. It hurts me so much more when I see him hurt. Much, much more.

Compassion

Finally, the fruit of this shift is that the energy that was wrapped up with the "me" is liberated and turns into an interest in serving and giving. The condition of the whole planet becomes *my* condition:

When this shift first happened, any little thing would make me cry—like the homeless in Santa Monica. Just yesterday, I was eating ice cream when I saw this lady getting trash from the trash cans. I couldn't continue eating my ice cream. We gave her money, and then I just wasn't hungry anymore. Then I started crying. I see everything that's happening in the world, and I feel very sad. There are so many battles happening, even within communities and cities. It is overwhelming.

HOW DO YOU GET THERE?

Let's revisit something important for a moment. The above portrait of qualities is just that: a description of how reality seems after the brain has been restored to its natural balance. It is not a recipe for how to precipitate the shift. In fact, very often it's the opposite of these qualities that offers the most fertile soil for awakening. When you are sick in bed, you could compare yourself with someone who is healthy. They are running around, going shopping, perhaps going dancing. Those are the results of feeling better, not the way to get better. The fastest way to recover from sickness is the opposite of those things: to stay in bed and to rest. Similarly, the qualities we have described are the symptoms of a shifted brain, not the path to it.

An awakened life may be characterized by bliss, but acting blissfully without real awakening just makes you a fake—better to fully feel the unmet pain. An awakened life may be characterized by trust, but to *pretend* to trust just makes you shallow, quoting new age bumper stickers—better to fully feel the fear. An awakened life may be characterized by intimacy with everything, but to fake that just creates entanglement and neediness—better to fully feel the loneliness.

From time to time, Bhagavan and the dasas have suggested some hints for the right kind of soil in which awakening can flourish. They have suggested that the practice of gratitude helps a great deal. They have often spoken of "staying with what is": fully feeling each thing as it arises, without trying to change it. And they have spoken of walking in presence, recognizing coincidences and grace in your life. But much more than any of these things, they emphasize that the choice is not ultimately in your hands.

Which brings us to the third criticism that has been aimed at the Oneness movement—the claim that enlightenment has to be given to you; there is nothing you can do from your side. Critics say that it creates a dependency on Amma and Bhagavan and expensive trips to India, and robs individuals of their own autonomy. Particularly in America, where Sinatra's "I Did It My Way" is the backup national anthem, people are very sensitive to the idea that anything is out of their hands. But still, we all know that there are some things one just cannot do for oneself. You cannot tickle yourself, or tell yourself a good joke, or give yourself a surprise gift, or perform brain surgery on yourself. Just like these things, Awakening into Oneness finally has to come as a gift of grace, because it is the final curtain call on the sense of a separate me being in charge. The shift happens when we take our hands off the steering wheel and open to grace.

The Oneness Blessing is the response of that grace to an open heart.

CHAPTER TWELVE

THE ONENESS BLESSING
AND THE GOLDEN AGE

Without a global revolution in the sphere of human consciousness, nothing will change for the better . . . and the catastrophe this world is headed toward—the ecological, social, demographic, or general breakdown of civilization—will be unavoidable."

This quote is not from Bhagavan nor Anandagiri nor your favorite spiritual author. These words were spoken in 1990 at a joint session of the United States Congress. The speaker was Václav Havel, the acclaimed playwright who became the first president of the Czech Republic.

Most everyone agrees that we are living at a pivotal time in human history. Some see it as the worst of times. Our entire global society and economy run on black sticky stuff that is in limited supply. What will happen when it runs out, no one knows. At the same time, the rate at which we are burning that sticky stuff is heating up the atmosphere of our planet, disrupting weather patterns, and potentially threatening all kinds of life forms—including us. Vast economic disparity; huge national debts; unprecedented power in the hands of global corporations bent on profiteering; corruption in government, business, and the media—the list is endless. We might have a chance to set some of these things right, were it not for the fact that so much of our collective energy is caught up in wars of fundamentalism. There are countless good reasons to feel that these are the worst of times and to lose hope.

And at the same time, as I explored at length in my previous book, *The Translucent Revolution*, there is plenty of reason to also see this as the best of times. A growing number of people in the world are displaying characteristics I described as "translucent"—that is, they are no longer limited to a private and self-centered agenda but have awakened to a deeper realization of interconnectedness. At the end of that book, I posed this question: Are there enough translucents—and has the transformation been deep enough—to precipitate a shift not only in a few people but also in the collective consciousness of the planet?

While Amma, Bhagavan, and all the dasas at the Oneness University speak of and focus a great deal on the Awakening into Oneness of individuals, the primary purpose and mission of everything they do is global.

On the surface, it might well seem like all the crises we face as a race are independent of each other. The only thing they seem to have in common is that we do not have solutions to any of them. Years ago, Albert Einstein reflected that you cannot solve any problem in the same state of consciousness in which it was created. Today, more and more people are recognizing that every crisis we face as a race is just another symptom of our current state of consciousness—a state that is unsustainable. Human beings have, for as long as we can remember, felt imprisoned in a sense of separation, trapped within the confines of the mind. We have gotten used to this situation; we regard it as the "normal" state of human life. But there is a growing recognition that this is not, in fact, *natural*—that we are all capable of something more. Anandagiri explains:

The vision of the Oneness University is that humanity can be set free. For Bhagavan, there is only one cause for human problems: the strong sense of a separate self, the sense of separateness, the feeling of a me and a not-me. There is no other kind of relationship that we know. We can only relate to things as the me and the not-me. This is what causes problems in the home and in relationships between people. And this is what causes problems between two nations or religious conflicts or any kind of problem. It is the sense of separateness or the feeling of the me and the not-me. Whatever our ideology, whatever virtues we practice, as long as we relate to our environment in this way, as the me and the not-me, conflict is unavoidable.

We will not achieve much by changing the system, because the system is not what is responsible for these problems. By changing or improving the system—whether religious, political, economic, or social—things might or might not improve. Working on the system is like working on the symptom, not the disease. The real cause, the root cause, is this sense of a separate self. Our present society is so preoccupied with the separate self, the individual is so strong, that it has to keep itself secure and safe, even at the expense of others, because that is the nature of the self. Unless that is addressed, it is impossible to expect a fundamentally different world.

Amma and Bhagavan's work is about addressing this problem. This is the purpose of deeksha, the Oneness Blessing: to work on the brain. By reducing the overactivity of the parietal lobes, this sense of self slowly starts disintegrating. You start feeling more and more connected, more and more one: at first with your family and your closer ones, and eventually with everything. Finally you begin to experience Oneness with all that is, Oneness with God. What Amma and Bhagavan are doing, this university, this movement, this deeksha, the teachings, the insights, is to help people right there. It is addressing the root of all the problems. Then, no matter what the system, there is going to be peace.

TIPPING POINT

At the Oneness University, they feel that this shift in collective consciousness could well happen in a relatively short time span. Although the physical manifestations of a new consciousness may take longer to show themselves as changes in the environment or political or economic structures, they feel that the shift needed in collective consciousness could well be in place in the next few years. Bhagavan explains that it has often come in revelations to the dasas, as well as to many participants in the longer courses in India, that the predominant frequency of human consciousness on this planet has the possibility to shift in the second decade of the twenty-first century, from preoccupation with separation to a collective awakening into Oneness.

The intervening years, according to Bhagavan, could be very rough or quite smooth—depending on our level of cooperation with the shift that is occurring in collective consciousness. If we resist the evolutionary leap we are being initiated into, we may experience considerable suffering. If we allow it, we will begin to enjoy a Golden Age.

A global shift of this kind has been anticipated in many different traditions. In India, for example, it is said that Kalki, the tenth incarnation of Vishnu, would appear at this time on a white horse and ride seven times around the planet to deliver humanity from separation into Oneness. Previous incarnations of Vishnu include Krishna and Rama. For several years, many Indian devotees called Bhagavan by the name Kalki and saw him as this incarnation. But more recently, Bhagavan explained that although this is indeed the time for this emergence, Kalki is not in fact one person but a collective awakening. Bhagavan speaks of the Oneness Blessing givers all over the world, and in a broader sense the entire field of awakening consciousness, as Kalki—as the new incarnation of divinity.

The same view has been shared by many others in recent years. Before the historical Buddha died, he reportedly predicted that a teacher named Maitreya would be the next to turn the wheel of dharma, twenty-five hundred years after the Buddha's death—which is right about now. The word *maitreya* literally means "the friend." Today, people like Vietnamese monk and author Thich Nhat Hanh feel that Maitreya has already come and is actively teaching in different incarnations all over the world. Today, it is the spirit of friendship that turns the wheel of dharma, the spirit of honest and open investigation into, and testimony to, the truth. It is the gathering itself that is the guru, friends meeting friends. In the same way, respected Christian theologians, like Father Alan Jones of Grace Cathedral and Bishop Richard Holloway of Edinburgh Cathedral, see the second coming of Christ as the emergence of the Christ consciousness in all of us.

The Swedish writer Carl Calleman, author of *The Mayan Calendar and the Transformation of Consciousness,* is one of the most respected living authorities on the Mayan calendar, which he sees as "a description of the evolution of consciousness." According to the calendar, the evolution of human consciousness can be mapped through a number of concentric levels, each of which comprises seven days and six nights. As the pattern unfolds, each higher level becomes shorter in time, the last of which began in 1999 and will cumulate in the fall of 2011. Calleman says:

Humanity is endowed with a certain number of filters blocking the perception of the divine and creating an illusion of separation. When we come to that end date, October 28, 2011, all these filters will be removed—which amounts to an experience of Oneness, of not being separate from the universe or from the divine. That's the time when a new field will become established on this planet. That doesn't mean that all the changes will happen on that particular day, but once the field is established, throughout time, action will manifest from this new field. This will happen probably most intensely throughout the year 2012 and then continue in various ways. As we come closer to this end date, the chances of awakening will increase to a point where the field favors this shift toward Oneness, a cosmic consciousness without separation from the divine.

MIDWIFING THE SHIFT

Bhagavan does not claim that they are creating this long-predicted shift in consciousness at Oneness University. Rather, he believes that the Oneness Blessing will help the brain to attune to the shift. It is rather like preparing for a monster wave. Handing out quality surfboards and lessons on how to use them could be the difference between drowning and, well, a truly awesome ride. Just as the most probable time line for the shift has been revealed to the dasas while in deep states of meditative absorption, so, too, have the ways that the Oneness movement can contribute to midwifing the shift been seen in visions.

First, the Oneness University hopes to train Oneness Blessing givers all over the world in the coming years. Together with the myriad of other magnificent contributions that are being made to create a translucent world, this may be enough to precipitate a global shift. At the time of this writing, some countries, like Sweden, with a population of nine-million people, already have several hundred Blessing givers. For the United States, there are almost a thousand Blessing givers at the time of this writing. India, with a population of more than a billion people, currently has seven thousand deeksha givers.

Because of the phenomenon of a "tipping point" mentioned earlier, only a relatively small percentage of the world's population needs to shift from separation to Oneness for the whole planet to shift. It may well be that the Oneness Blessing proves to be a highly efficacious way to lubricate this process, which is occurring anyway.

Bhagavan suggests that as we move closer to a global tipping point, the effect of the Oneness Blessing will get stronger and quicker. He predicts that in the last phase, just one three-minute Blessing will precipitate enough of a shift for the brain to become attuned to the new vibration of Oneness. It may not be needed for this to happen individually. Already, large Oneness conventions are happening all over the world, where thousands of people receive the Oneness Blessing at the same time. Attendees report that the effect of the collective Blessings is much stronger than when it is given one-on-one.

Second, a number of people, almost all in India at this point, are moving into much deeper states than what we have already described as an Awakening into Oneness. At the Oneness University, these people are called "cosmic beings," and their presence and Blessings have been the single greatest catalyst to precipitate awakening in others. They are not only awakened; they have also become completely entrenched in the divine, to such an extent that some of them do not speak or involve themselves in normal life at all. Many of them resonate with a specific frequency of the divine, which comes through their Blessings. So, from one, you might experience the quality of Jesus through the Blessing; from another, you might experience Buddha, or Mother Mary, or Mira.

The power of sitting with these beings is extraordinary. When Chameli and I first visited, we were invited to sit with about fifteen of them in a small hall. The silence seemed to soak through one's skin and penetrate every part of one's being. It was as if an irresistible magnet were pulling all of us into deep stillness. Many who have had this opportunity report that they felt huge shifts happening in the physical brain, as though fingers were moving inside the skull and massaging different areas of the brain from the inside. Some found that they were so absorbed in silence and divine presence after a half hour sitting, they felt completely filled, unable to move for a while, initiated into a completely different reality. Thoughts would stop completely or recede as though into a far-off room, leaving the perception of the moment untouched. Colors would become bright and luminous; sounds around one would seem as though they were happening within the body itself. Every month, more people are transitioning into cosmic beings—drawn into a life of continuous prayer, meditation, and communion with the divine—and initiating this experience in others.

Which leads us to the third aspect of how the Oneness University is helping to midwife the shift in global consciousness: the Oneness Temple. On a forty-two-acre plot at the heart of the Oneness University, an extraordinary structure has been built over the past several years. The Oneness Temple stands 108 feet high, with a total area of 112,000 square feet. It has three floors, the highest of which has no internal pillars—making it, at the time of this writing, the largest hall without internal pillars in Asia.

Before it was ever built, many people had dreams and visions of this structure. The architect who drew the plans says that it just came "through" him, without much thinking at all. Bhagavan and many of the dasas and visitors have had visions of, once the building is completed, eight thousand cosmic beings sitting at all times in the upper pillarless hall, generating a "coherent field" of consciousness. In their visions, some have seen visitors coming into the upper hall for a few minutes at a time to attune themselves to this morphic field. Some have seen that, unlike most temples, which are dedicated to a particular deity, this temple will be dedicated to the one divine presence that is everywhere. In such visions, when people from any faith come and worship, they see a sign of their God's presence in the temple. They pray in any fashion they want, and they see their own image of God.

What is not simply a vision, but an enormous and impressive reality, is that the structure is already nearing completion. At the time of this writing, many of the other buildings in the same campus have been completed and are being used. All the structural work on the temple has been completed, and the outside of the temple has been largely covered in white marble, leaving only the interior marble work to be completed. Quite possibly by the time you are reading this, the temple will have been finished, and we will have discovered which of these visions became an actuality.

Bhagavan explains that he sees the temple as the powerhouse behind the work the Oneness University is doing to support the shift in global consciousness:

When eight thousand people are sitting close to each other in that building, it is the equivalent of a much greater number if they were disbursed all over the world. With that many beings, at that level of consciousness, it's a great boost to the global Awakening into Oneness across the planet. The temple belongs to the whole of humanity. It is something like a powerhouse, generating the power for deeksha givers distributed across the world. They will receive the power and retransmit it.

Through these three factors—the training of Oneness Blessing givers, the spontaneous transformation of many people to become "cosmic beings," and the construction of the temple—it is anticipated that the Oneness Blessing will get deeper and deeper over the next years. Many of the Blessing givers I interviewed for this book reported that they have already noticed this to be the case, that as this whole integrated plan unfolds, people get deeper results from the Oneness Blessing every month.

THE GOLDEN AGE

All we have ever known of life is separation, lived through the filters of the mind. All that our history records is stories of life lived in the same way. We have small hints here and there—in the events around the life of the Buddha, for example, or in some ancient myths—of another way, but these seem remote from the life that we know. I asked Bhagavan what sort of world he foresees emerging in the next years:

This is the time when the whole of humanity could easily become enlightened. We are going to see the emergence of a new world order, a new kind of spirituality, a new kind of government, a new kind of educational system. Everything is going to change because there is going to be a new human being: totally different in his thought, in the way he functions. Humanity will become like one family, where people are cooperating and not competing. Once cooperation starts, all good things are going to happen. The very experience of existence can be very, very different: full of joy and happiness. How could joyous, happy people create a miserable world? It's just not possible. So it's going to be a great new world.

He went on to expand on this vision as it might affect specific arenas of human activity:

Politics

There will be people who will have been totally transformed, no longer engaging in self-centered activities, because the sense of a separate self will be gone. They will only live for the whole of humanity. These are the people who will be in politics—politicians who are not self-centered, who are not narrow-minded. We will see bureaucrats and technicians, spiritual leaders and people in business, who are no longer self-centered, but rather like one big family. Everybody working for the other. We expect things to change very dramatically in politics. Power will come down to the common person, so power will belong to everybody. Decisions could be made in a collective way.

Peace

There is war in the world because someone here and there and his wife are not at peace, because they fight with each other. That's all there is to it. Because we have conflict as individuals, we have violence. This ultimately becomes conflict between nations. It may be difficult to see that. That is why we focus on relationship here. If we knock out all conflicts in human beings, there cannot be war or violence. It is impossible.

As relationships fall in order, you will find there are fewer calamities in the world, less disease, less war. If we really want to handle war, we must look at our own relationships, which means to look at ourselves. There is no use looking at violence there—look at the violence within you. The harsh words you utter, when you hurt somebody—sometimes speaking politely, but hurting all the same. All this is violence; we are a violent species. We do all these things, and we create our own little nations—it is very tribalistic. Once all this is transformed, there will the Golden Age. There will be no nations as such, no countries as such. We will be just one humanity.

The Role of Women

We will see a very balanced spirituality no longer based on beliefs but on the actual experience of God. I don't think you can call God either masculine or feminine, so these distinctions will just disappear. In the university here, men and women play an equal role. Amma and I have an equal status; no one is superior to the other. We have female acharyas and male acharyas, female and male dasas, and, in general, the females outnumber the males. It is a strongly feminine order. The emergence of the awakened feminine will influence politics, education—everything will be influenced in this way, because there has to be a balance of the masculine and the feminine. At the helm of affairs are going to be women.

Religion

There are nearly seven billion people on this planet; they can experience God in seven billion ways. People are different; they're constructed differently; their perceptions are going to be different. That is why there are so many religions. The world can never be unified under one common religion or under one common faith or under one common principle. The world needs different religions. But if we can have direct experience of what our religions talk about, if they are not just beliefs or mere words, then nobody needs to be taught virtue or love; it will be our natural state and experience.

The Environment

There is a close correlation between human consciousness and the physical processes occurring on the planet. Soon we will realize that the earth is a living organism that we depend on like a mother. You can speak to Mother Earth. You'll be amazed to see that she is a being who can talk to you. She could tell you about her pains and what she is going through. She is not just dead earth or something that has no spirit. She is a being, a very powerful being

The moment conflict levels are reduced in human consciousness, we will find dramatic changes in the earth level also. You will find a reduction in insects, in pests, in floods, and in volcanic eruptions. All these things are a natural consequence of the reduction of conflict in human consciousness, because there is such a close relation between the two. In some villages, when we do programs, there is a transformation and immediately there is rain. It had not rained for four or five years. And then there is a downpour, and the crops are plentiful. There are fewer insects coming, fewer pests. Everything in nature responds immediately.

We are part of evolution, we are part of nature, and so we should cooperate. Nature expects us to cooperate. We need to give it a helping hand.

If you read a vision such as this right after reading the paper or watching the evening news, it could sound very unrealistic. Relative to the state of the world today and the rate at which change has occurred for humankind in the past, it *is* unrealistic—particularly considering that this is not a vision for another century, but for our lifetime. There are three factors that we can bear in mind before dismissing all this out of hand.

First, Bhagavan presents this as a vision of what must happen for humanity to survive. It is a possibility, not a certainty:

As far as the dasas and I are concerned, we are sure it can happen because that is what we have seen. But the problem with seeing the future is that the future is full of possibilities, and we are always seeing just one. From that point of view, you may say we are being optimistic. We don't want to look into other possibilities; we want to look into this possibility only. But by all of us coming together, working together, there is every chance it's going to happen.

Second, like many other visionaries today, he recognizes that the very crisis itself quickens awakening. We are more inclined to wake up when we are tossed around in a nightmare. When we are cocooned in a cozy dream, on the other hand, we are more inclined to go on sleeping.

But the last factor is by far the most compelling. You might recall what Dr. Bruce Lipton and Dr. Craig Wagstaff had to say about spontaneous healings and remissions in Chapter Five. When we are caught in a mechanical view of the body, there are limited options available. The factors that contribute to disease take time to slowly develop, and so the process of healing will also take time—step by slow step—because A causes B and B causes C and C causes D. In a quantum relationship to the body, none of that applies anymore; miracles become normal. Cancer disappears overnight; the blind get to see again; the lame throw away their crutches. The shift in global consciousness that Bhagavan proposes, and that countless other visionaries also see as essential for humanity's survival, is not a change from one state of affairs to another. It is a transformational leap out of the collective mind that we know. It is a leap from the limits of a cause-and-effect Newtonian world into a quantum universe, where everything is possible—where the global caterpillar becomes a butterfly.

It may be that this quantum leap in consciousness is happening now simply because this is the time, because everything that has occurred for you and for me and for all of humanity has led us to the point where there is no other future but this one. In our six and a half hours of interviews, I asked Bhagavan for some words to sum up his message to humanity:

Some people have said it takes eons to become enlightened. I would say you have already been around for eons. The preparation is over.

Now is the time for us to really make it. We have been building a huge mansion over the last few million years. I think the time has now come to enter the mansion. And I'm full of hope that we are going to make it. People should not lose hope, and people should not be too distressed. You can be quite positive about the future of humanity and the planet, because this huge shift in consciousness is only a few years away. And the more confident you are, the more definitely it is going to happen.

A new civilization is taking birth. I won't say it's going to happen. I say it is already taking birth.

CHAPTER THIRTEEN

THE
ONENESS PROCESS

As you leave the main highway that runs from Chennai in the south to Calcutta in the northeast, the turnoff to Varadaiah-palem takes you by surprise. Just like Platform 9¾, where Harry Potter boards the train to Hogwarts, you could easily miss it if you did not know what you were looking for. The driver has to find a break in the center divide, double back on his tracks for a few hundred feet, and then slip suddenly between a tobacco stall and a place selling samosas. After following a narrow road for a while, dodging between cows and geese and people everywhere, you suddenly emerge out into rural India, as though having time-traveled back a few hundred years. For a country with more than a billion people in an area one-third the size of the United States, it is amazing that there can be so much open space here, with so few vehicles. There's just the local herd of goats, tended by an old toothless man; an occasional hawk in the sky; and vast open spaces that seem to exist just the way God planned them.

The Oneness Temple looms up on you from far away. Even if you know it is coming, it still takes you by surprise. It seems like the most ancient and, at the same time, the most modern structure imaginable, something between a palace from Vedic mythology and a flying saucer. On the other side of the road is the campus known as Golden City Campus Two, where the Oneness Processes are offered for non-Indian participants. My wife and I did not stay at this campus when we first visited, for there is another campus for writers, teachers, and others who have been invited as guests. So, one evening, we went to visit. The campus comprises two white, single-story halls at one end, each several thousand square feet, which house the teaching and dining halls. At the other end of the campus are two three-story buildings where the participants stay—one building for the men and one for the women. In between is a spacious lawn.

This campus is for non-Indian visitors to train to give the Oneness Blessing. Indian nationals, with quite different psyches and needs, undergo a different kind of training. Courses have been offered here every month continuously since 2004 to groups from every country in the world, ranging from sixty to six hundred at a time. A course for Americans had just started a few days before we visited. We sat with a group of male dasas from India in a smaller meeting room upstairs in the men's building. All of them were between twenty-five and thirty years old, each responsible for between twenty and forty participants. We met with them after the participants had retired for the night, around ten o'clock. They were all still ready to party.

It was a remarkable experience to sit with those seven young men. They really defy any attempt at categorization. Although they now live as monks, they are no strangers to the ways of the world. Murali studied to be a doctor and lived for several years in Russia. Krishnaraj is an accomplished musician, who has recorded several CDs. Srinivas studied as an engineer, while Rajesh and Radhakrishna have studied commerce. Despite the fact that it was late and they had been up since four in the morning and faced a similar start the next morning, they were all totally alive, cracking jokes and discussing the answers to my questions in their native Telugu before agreeing together on the best answer. They were all completely unique individuals, and yet they spoke with one voice, always coming into agreement with one another before moving on to another topic. We will hear from them here as that one voice.

Each course is uniquely designed by the dasas themselves. They have all passed through their own process of Awakening into Oneness, and they have all faced their own shadow sides—so they know what to expect. Each dasa has responsibility for a certain area of the world: Radhakrishna keeps in touch with the Oneness Blessing givers in the United States, for example, while Krishnaraj has responsibility for Europe. They are continually in touch with people there by phone and e-mail. In this way, they are able to monitor the effects of the course after people get home and to make adjustments for each successive course accordingly.

It is an evolving process. It changes from one process to the next, depending on how the phenomenon is growing and how people are responding. The process evolves from the insights of the people, because we can get the feel of how humanity is progressing from the process itself.

This brings us to another of the criticisms commonly aimed at the Oneness University: these guys just can't make up their minds about anything! When I was in India, Anandagiri took me on a tour of the Jeevashram school, several hours away from Oneness University. "This is where Bhagavan and Amma stayed while the school was open," he announced as we entered one building. Then half an hour later, he showed me another room, "This was Amma and Bhagavan's room." Then another and another. After about six of these announcements, I shared my confusion with him. He grinned at me sheepishly, "They moved around a lot!" Nothing in the world around Amma and Bhagavan stays the same for very long—not even their names. If you go for even a superficial Web cruise, you will find that Bhagavan has been called Kalki, Mukteshwar, and several other names. The organization itself has shifted from the Golden Age Foundation to the Foundation for Global Awakening to the Oneness Movement to the Oneness University. Even as I was preparing this manuscript for publication, more changes of vocabulary were in the works.

Critics view this tendency toward constant change as being shifty and unreliable, like an offshore trust that is here today and gone tomorrow. To the dasas, on the other hand, this is simply the nature of things. "The only thing that does not change on this Earth is change itself." Nothing structural or organizational is held sacred by Amma, Bhagavan, or the dasas. When I asked Bhagavan about this tendency to change vocabulary so regularly, his response was that he simply wants to awaken the world, and he is happy to adopt any structure, vocabulary, or appearance to get the job done. He has no problem changing anything at any time, as he has absolutely no interest in dogma whatsoever. And so it is that the courses continue to shift and change and be taken apart and reconstructed as the participants change, as the quality of collective consciousness changes, and as the dasas find out more and more about the dark secrets of the Western psyche.

The dasas pass through the process with the participants every time:

Every month when they come, they do not know what to expect. So we, too, start fresh. We do not know what is going to happen, either. As they move into looking at relationships, we move into relationships. We go through the process with them all day, every day. We travel their journey with them. We get in touch with their pain, with whatever they are undergoing. Since we have undergone the same journey some years ago, we know exactly what it is.

Since the Oneness Blessing has the power to release old hurts and memories, participants often pass through strong emotions or become upset during the program. I looked at these serene monks sitting before me, cross-legged on the bamboo mats, and wondered how they would fare with an irate New Yorker or an outraged German:

Sometimes participants get frustrated. Then we hold their hands and pray for grace. Whatever they experience, we look at them, and it is very clear that it is a part of their process. Something is getting triggered in them. There is no way you can reason it out with them, because maybe the child in them is surfacing, or some hurt memory is coming up. There is no way you can tell them it will be all right. The only thing you can do is to go with them. We pay attention to them, we listen to them, and, in that, things get solved.

When we listen to them in the presence, somehow it is all automatic. In fact, many times we experience what's going on in them. It all happens. Grace comes. Grace is here the whole time they are here. So it happens. We are not disturbed by it, because the fact that these things are coming out means that something good is happening. We have seen it in our own lives. We have experienced our own anger, our own doubts, our own questions.

To put it very simply, when people come for a process, they have certain ideas. When they are going through beautiful experiences of love and tranquility and all this, they think they are in a process. When they move into frustration and anger and guilt, they think they are out of the process. That is the problem. When we look at the people, it is clear to us that nothing is not a process; everything is the Oneness process. Whether they go into guilt or whether they go into love, both are the process. So we are perfectly at ease even if a person comes and says, "I feel like killing you. I feel like running out of this place, and I don't want to look at all of you people." We know that is a process for him. And he has to go through it.

COMPONENTS OF THE ONENESS PROCESS

Although every course is different and designed from scratch by the dasas themselves in response to previous experiences, there are certain elements that have been common to every course from the beginning. These are the building blocks that rearrange themselves each time to create a new and unique experience. In no particular order, they are as follows:

Silence

Participants talk for the first two or three days in order to meet their roommates and get to know each other, but for the majority of the time, they are encouraged to be with themselves, to avoid using chatter as a means of escape.

Men and Women Are Separated

Even for the married couples, men and women sleep in different buildings and usually undergo the process in different meeting halls. At meal times, they see each other:

We have seen that when they are in a group together or left to talk, their progress is much less profound. When we ask them to keep their distance, we have found that it goes much, much deeper. When the women are separate, they have much greater freedom to express themselves on certain topics. When the men are left together, given freedom of expression, they understand each other.

There are usually about twice as many women as men enrolled in any one course.

Preparing for Awakening

No matter what is happening, the Oneness Process is always in some way creating a fertile soil for the Awakening into Oneness. According to the dasas:

The whole process creates an atmosphere for awakening to happen. It depends on many factors, and each person proceeds at their own speed toward whatever final fulfillment they are searching for. The process both initiates the journey and catalyzes it, by providing the right kind of insights, the right kind of teachings, and the shifts in the brain. A leap in consciousness happens in its own time. The way they experience things—getting used to that new level of consciousness, working from that level, and seeing things in that way permanently—depends on many factors, including the body, what has happened in the past, and the surroundings in which they are living. But the process initiates the whole journey, it pushes them into this beautiful journey of Oneness, in a powerful way so that they don't go back. It pushes them upward.

If we use the word "enlightenment," people immediately think about a particular station. They think of an end point, a milestone. They say, "Okay, I've done that. It's over for me." Actually, it's the beginning; the journey actually begins from there. This is the journey, jumping into God. After that, the journey is endless. But the beauty is that, as you move in the endless journey, the movement itself is joy, and the movement itself is peace.

Energy Experiences

This journey into Oneness is usually punctuated by strong energy experiences, manifesting as intense heat moving up the spine or as energy moving through and filling the whole body. Some people have visions of deities or are overcome with waves of emotion: tears, devotion, or laughter. All these experiences, which are commonplace in the course and happen each and every day, have the effect of opening up the energy circuits (or *nadis*) in the body, opening the chakras, and making the whole system receptive to divine energy.

Preparing to Give the Oneness Blessing

Although participants leave the course able to give the Oneness Blessing, there is really no technique involved, no skill to master. It is not something that you do; it's more something that does *you,* once you have been sufficiently prepared. All the components of the course—the presence of the dasas, the silence, receiving so many Blessings, the insights and experiences—contribute to a clearing of the channels. One day, lo and behold, you are invited to give Blessings to another, and the Blessing is flowing through you, too.

The Moola Mantra

Just like a movie with a memorable soundtrack, the entire course in India takes place to a sacred mantra, the melody and words of which are unique to this specific transmission. Like so many things here, this mantra came to several of the dasas at the same time as a revelation. No one ever thought about it or made a decision to compose it. The mantra infuses the course so completely that, when one returns home to the daily bustle, one only needs to sing it or hear it a few times for the energy of the course to be invoked once again.

Om Satchitananda Parabrahma
Purushothama Paramatma
Sri Bhagavati Sametha
Sri Bhagavate Namaha

Bhagavan explains the meaning:

First there is existence, intelligence, and bliss—satchitananda. That is the source of all things. This becomes part of parabrahma, *the next level of manifestation. It becomes the universe. This parabrahma becomes* purushothama, *the One Being, which is the next stage of evolution.* Paramatma *is the indweller in everybody that controls and moves the creation. That manifests in living beings, the masculine and feminine incarnation of the divine. The mantra is an evolution in consciousness, reflecting how, in stages, the one becomes the many.*

Darshan

At the time of this writing, participants in the Oneness Process sit once with Amma in silent meditation, and one or more times with Bhagavan. Remember that everything changes with every course! It is during these periods of silent communion, called darshan, that many participants remember their most powerful energetic shifts and breakthroughs.

Schedule

The day starts soon after dawn with a session of meditation, singing, and prayer. After a break for breakfast, the participants reconvene around ten in the morning and meet until lunchtime. During this time, there are Oneness Blessings, teachings, and sometimes other practices. There is often a long break for lunch and rest, and then another session from four in the afternoon until eight at night, when the program finishes with dinner.

• • •

This brings us to the last of the criticisms commonly aimed at the Oneness Movement: Why is the Oneness Process so expensive? At the time of this writing, people in Western countries pay US$5,500 to attend the course—which is, of course, considerably more than it costs to run such a program in a third-world country like India. So where does all the money go? Since this is probably the most common criticism leveled at the entire phenomenon, I took it upon myself to play detective to see if anyone could be found sitting by the pool sipping banana daiquiris and stashing the money for dubious motives. I have done my best to offer you some dirt here, but I have come up empty-handed thus far.

The first thing to know is that a great deal more money has been spent in the last few years by the Oneness University than has been brought in. The temple site alone, with all its adjacent buildings, cost more than US$17 million to build. All the extensive work that has been done in the 140 villages around Varadaiahpalem has been done for free. Moreover, the higher price Western participants pay may cover some of the costs of attendees from poorer nations, as participants from Africa, Russia, Indonesia, and India pay much less—sometimes nothing at all. There is also a scholarship program for Western visitors who have a proven track record of service and who come recommended.

I have met all the key players involved in the university. Without exception, they live quite modestly. The last time we visited there, we were picked up at the airport in a red passenger van, about a year old, the kind of vehicle that might be used to transport school children or employees of a company on a field trip. The next day, the same vehicle was used to drive Bhagavan to visit Amma at Nemam. He was living in exactly the same-size room, in the same kind of building, as where we were staying. Anandagiri and Samadarshini who between them, run most of the programs there, sleep in dormitories with the other monks. Interestingly, all the criticism of the university for charging too much money has come from people who have never been there. I have yet to meet a single person who has taken the course and felt that it was money ill spent.

Bhagavan himself was unequivocal with me that he did not see the Oneness Process as lasting for more than a few years:

We are aiming for the complete abolition of the course itself. We want humanity to be liberated, not to be conducting courses forever. This is just a preparation for the people who will give deeksha, and then the whole of humanity will step into a new phase. That is why this order of dasas may well not exist soon. Otherwise, it would become a cult; it would become a religion. We are thinking that in a few years, once the mission is achieved, there will be a winding up of the show, and the dasas will go back to lead their anonymous lives. We are very clear about it.

THE PROGRESSION OF THE COURSE

Each of the three weeks of the Oneness Process has a specific focus or theme. Although the course as a whole is one integral experience, and although anything can happen at any time, these three phases have been common to every course to date.

Week One: Samskara Shuddhi

The first week focuses on your personal life: your relationship with your parents, your family, your past, and yourself. This process of deep clearing is often referred to as *samskara shuddhi,* or the washing away of psychological impressions. It is a healing of the heart. The aim of this week is not to change or improve the personality or personal history, but to bring participants to see themselves as they are, as they have been. The dasas explain:

> *We have images as masks that we identify with, so we miss out on our true nature. Our emphasis in the first week is on self-acceptance. One can hate oneself, feel guilt for the past. Many people are not able to accept their past. They review their life, and often they see how much they have hurt others. The Oneness Blessings help them to feel exactly what the other person felt. When we are not comfortable with what we are, with who we are, we constantly try blending in. We lose energy; we hate ourselves. Because we hate ourselves, we try to do something to make other people love us. It is all because of not being able to bear what we are. Helping the participants to work on this results in self-acceptance, loving oneself as you are now. If you can't love yourself, how can you love others or expect others to love you? The same is true with the divine. Many people have a concept of a punishing God that arises from their own self-hate and guilt. After the Blessing, their view of God changes naturally into a more compassionate and friendly God.*

Samskara shuddhi can take many forms, and one is not presented as any better than another. For some participants, it is simply a gentle seeing, a liberation and deep experiencing of themselves as they are. For others, it involves more outward expressions: one may pass through periods of weeping, while another vents anger and frustration. All participants ultimately experience the same result. Particular emphasis is put on the birth process, so that many are able to reexperience the time spent in the womb and pass through their own birth again.

The space is different from the psychological work some people have done in the past. It is not just bringing things to the surface; it is filling the void with love. That is where grace enters. Whatever is released, there is a love being filled from presence. The connection with the presence is very, very important in this stage—recognizing the presence and connecting to the presence. That is how they move into joy; that is how they move naturally into forgiveness.

We do not do much to make this happen. The process itself runs on grace, like everything that happens to you. All we do is hold an intention, and the process is designed in such a way that will bring grace into action. If the whole gathering has taken an intent together, the atmosphere will help to spread it. The whole campus will respond— not just the people, but the dog, the bird, the sun, the cloud, the truck outside, the person working with the food that day.

In the process of researching this book, I heard literally hundreds of stories of transformation from this period of samskara shuddhi. There are more than enough personal testimonies to fill a *Chicken Soup for the Soul* book, and perhaps some day they will. Below are a couple of random examples. See the Resources section for websites where you can read even more.

Clementine is an African-American woman. Her experience is typical of how lifelong patterns can come to the surface in the first week and then be liberated through the Oneness Blessing. From the very beginning of the course, she always wanted to sit right in the front. She would arrive half an hour before the session would start in order to get a good seat. She would ask many questions every time, and if her questions were not taken before the others, she would become offended and emotional. The dasas never tried to change this in her. Growing up as an African-American woman, she had suffered a lot. One day, all of this came to the surface. Someone else arrived before her, and she lost her usual place right in the front. She became convinced that the dasas were prejudiced against black people. That same day, a Blessing was given for participants to remember their worst fears. Some worked with fears of heights or of violence. Clementine had a memory of when she was very young, traveling on a bus. She was sitting at the front and was taken by the white people and thrown to the back of the bus. She was so hurt that she made a decision in that moment that all her life no one would send her to the back ever again. "I will sit at the front. Always." She became the head nurse, always the leader in whatever she was doing. Through the energy of the Blessing that day, she was able to fully feel the pain she had felt in the bus all those years ago, and the pattern got broken.

Kelvin's experience is typical of many other stories and shows us the difference between true self-acceptance and simply trying to fix ourselves. He had many strong experiences before his twenty-one-day course began, but once he arrived in India, nothing seemed to be happening. He felt frustrated. His frustration turned slowly into feelings of pain and anger. "I felt like I was wearing many layers of clothes, like there was a brick wall all around me. I didn't want to be there anymore. My girlfriend told me we had to leave there and then, or she would break up with me. I wanted to go." The dasas just told him to fully experience what he was going through, and everything would be fine. But all that kept coming for him was the feeling of not being good enough:

One night I sat alone there and reflected, "I am not a good person. I have done all kinds of horrible things in my life; things have been endlessly troublesome." All kinds of feelings arose, feelings I have had all my life: "No one cares for me. I am not good enough. People don't love me or respect me for what I am." I felt like a septic tank. Not only the septic tank, but also the waste in the tank. It was really a terrible place to be in, to continuously feel there is no one for me, that nobody loves me or cares for me. What I saw and felt there was absolutely shocking, and I didn't know how to get out of it.

Then I remembered one of the dasa's words: "The suffering and pain is self-generated; you can blame no one for it, not your parents, friends, no one!" As this came back to me, I realized, "Okay! So perhaps I am the waste and the septic tank and all the horrible things that could ever be, but who cares? I have done all these terrible things, but so what? I didn't build this wall around me, so obviously I can't break my way through it." I realized that nothing was actually within my control, and so I needed to do nothing. I gave up, and that was it. I sat back, and after that, nothing seemed to matter. Nothing could really bother me. I realized, "This is who I am. I can't change it; who I am right now is who I am. If I am bad, I am bad; if I am good, so be it." It became clear that there is no good, no bad—these are just words. There is no evil, no sacred, because they are all illusions. Once I saw I could do nothing, I was free. I slept beautifully the whole night. The next morning, I felt so liberated. My face, body language, and outlook had all changed completely. I felt totally free and easy at every single step, and every moment of every day since that night.

Once I gave it all up, everything started to happen. My face changed. I felt so good inside, and I started to experience divine presence. Now if people want to say something that insults me, who cares? It is, after all, a word or two. Just let it go through, and it's gone. I might be upset for a minute or two, or even five minutes or even half a day, but so what? They are not upsetting me; I am only upsetting myself.

Week Two: Awakening to Reality

The dasas explain that while the first week is an opportunity to experience and express everything that has been trapped within the mind, the second week allows one to transcend the mind, to see it for what it is. They explain this as a shift from a worm's-eye view to a bird's-eye view:

They recognize their perceptions and their assumptions about life, about reality, about God, about self. As they recognize their assumptions, they are released from them. They start seeing things from a different, higher perception. And that is freedom.

They start to recognize the nature of thought, the nature of life, the nature of mind, the nature of a person. And so they shift from an "uh-huh" experience to an "aha!" experience. What is enlightenment? It is simply a shift in perception leading to a shift in reality. The process is no longer about them questioning and trying to get somewhere; rather, the second week shows them how the presence of the divine views life. In that higher perspective, things begin to dissolve. These assumptions that are so hard, making you see life in a very tough way, become softer.

We question the whole idea of being a person. We look systematically at the thoughts, the body, the personalities, everything that constitutes the sense of existence. As you go step by step, restructuring your sense of existence, you start seeing that you don't exist independently but are part of the whole universe, part of the divine. You see that the thoughts are not your thoughts but part of the ancient mind, and that the sense of separation is more of an illusion—what is time is actually interconnectedness.

When we help them see things as they are, naturally, instantly almost, suffering vanishes. When you start experiencing things as they are, there is just joy. There is just freedom. We help them discover that, with the help of grace.

As they begin to see that thoughts are not theirs, or the body is not in their control, that their personalities are arising spontaneously, they discover that everything is interconnected, and the whole universe is influencing them. Naturally, the sense of a controller that is participating in this process and making them happen begins to appear futile. They become more of a witness to all this. They begin to have this experience of staying out of the mind, removing the resistance to what it is, what life is. Rather than trying to push things away, they start to flow. They see that there's a flow going on. Once you've seen that, you become the flow. There is no suffering. Personal suffering is gone.

Philip was also very frustrated for a great deal of the twenty-one-day Oneness Process, because nothing was happening. Other people were having powerful emotional and energetic experiences, but he was having nothing. He went to two darshans with Bhagavan and was not impressed. He felt nothing. After the darshan with Amma, he felt his heart opening for the first time, and he prayed to be able to feel his anger completely. He went to bed feeling unwell.

The next morning they were meditating and singing the Moola Mantra together. He explains:

Something happened there, something very, very deep. On the way back, I realized that I had no thought. No thought at all. I was just walking. I was looking at the stones on the ground, but it was not me; it was the presence. The presence was looking at the stones. The feet were walking, and the presence was looking at all the details. As the presence was looking, I asked myself, "What is there if there is no anger, if there is no sadness, if there is no pain? What remains?" Then I started to laugh and laugh. The answer came so rapidly: Nothing. There is nothing. People suffer so much in pain and have so many negative feelings, but there is nothing here; there is just nothing! Everything I had seen, everything that we had covered in the course, suddenly became real. In one second, everything got clear. "This body is not my body. There is no thought. The personality is just arising on its own." They had been telling us for two weeks that there was nothing there. But it's true—there is nothing at all. For the rest of the day, the presence was just experiencing every detail. It was like emerging again as a newborn baby, just watching the beautiful details of life around me.

Philip's experience is typical of many who have taken the process. Even though it may have seemed that nothing was happening for him, all the Blessings brought him to the point where he was able, for the first time, to question the deepest assumptions of the mind. The confinement to a sense of a separate self was broken instantaneously, and he realized that the sense of a "me" separate from existence is just an illusion. As you may well know, this realization has been regarded for millennia as the essence of enlightenment.

Week Three: Awakening to God

The third week is all about becoming one with the divine. There is even less teaching; there is simply a dissolving into the divine presence. The whole course leads up to living in the presence, living with the presence. There is an altar in the hall where the course takes place. On that altar, you can see every kind of image of the divine, and the participants are encouraged to put their own pictures there. The Christians come and put an image of Christ; the Muslims place their sacred text or the names of Allah. Buddhists might bring a Buddha statue, and Hindus could bring any one of a pantheon of deities. Some people feel the divine in nature, and they place flowers, rocks, or part of a tree on the altar. Many people feel the divine in Amma and Bhagavan, and so they put their picture there. Whatever image of the divine people feel connected with, the third week of the course will deepen that connection. The transformation that has occurred in the first two weeks leads many people to question the idea they have of God. Many discover that their perception of the divine has been clouded by their judgments of people or by the shame and guilt they feel about themselves.

"That is why we say 'Design your own God,'" says Bhagavan:

Masculine or feminine or both, friendly or tough, one who will quickly answer your prayers or take a long time to answer, one who might need strong worship or a careful choice of prayer or just a friendly chat—we suggest that you design this consciously. Most people design an image of God according to their personality. First make some changes to your own personality; then design a God that will really work. If you are a very angry person yourself, and you're trying to create a very gentle God, it may not work. Being an angry person, you might also have to create an angry God. The way you experience God depends on you.

He goes on to explain that God itself has no form. It is neither masculine nor feminine; it is the source of everything material, mental, emotional, and spiritual, and it can take any form according to the conditioning of the devotee. So like it or not, we all unconsciously create our own God. After all the clearing and awakening of the first two weeks, the third week of the course allows that creation of the personal God to become conscious, to become alive and vibrant.

So much poetry has emerged out of this last week of the Oneness Process. The participants start to feel the Oneness energy flowing through them. In addition to the hands-on Oneness Blessing that they are giving and receiving together, they may start to discover music, art, writing, flowing in a river of devotion to the myriad forms of the divine mystery.

Here is Phillipe Devos, a Sufi teacher from France:

I was listening to the voice of my mother and the Om. I felt I was a newborn baby, one with everything, with the animals and trees, changing color and light. My Sufi practice was growing deeper. I had a dream. The prophet asked me to sit down, and fed me so tenderly with his own fingers. I was kissing his fingers when he put the food in my mouth. This was proof to me that this beautiful gift was from God.

Here is Sheila Holloway from Canada:

I was lying in my bed, and I had a vision of Jesus standing at the end of my bed. He was calling my name. He called it so clearly, like it was a whisper. It wasn't any Jesus that I recognized. He was very dark-skinned. He had hazel eyes and long brown hair and the most beautiful robe that I've ever seen, of the softest fabric. I could feel the fabric touching me, as though I went through the fabric, and the fabric went through me. It was the most stunningly beautiful feeling. The heart opened up, and I became Him and He became me.

Then everybody became one. Jesus was one; we were all one. I was everybody, and everybody was me. And the tears just started flowing from my eyes. I didn't know who I was anymore. Everything was me. Even the flies were so beautiful they could land on my face, and I just wanted to kiss them. They felt so beautiful.

I went outside, and I was the sky; the sky was me. Every person I saw, I became that person, and they became me. I didn't know there was such a thing as that kind of love. I loved everybody I saw. And I don't mean just that I loved them. There was such a sense of compassion. I saw the dogs and felt so compassionate toward them. Before, I had paid no attention to them whatsoever. And the workers that I saw on the building, they were all one. There was such a sense of oneness. Absolute and total oneness.

Here is Dr. Rahasya Fritjof Kraft, a medical doctor and spiritual teacher from Germany:

This was a totally new experience, that the divine can be directly experienced through this body-mind in different forms. I had amazing experiences with Christ, and even with Ganesha, with Shiva, with Quanyin, with Lautzu, with Bodhidharma. It gave me an internal view of how this level of consciousness sees the world. It left a deeper insight into the magic of our existence in this world. It opened a lot of doors. I am a very pragmatic person; I don't believe in esoteric experiences unless I experience them. But I had such unbelievable direct experiences of divine beings entering and showing me the qualities in this body. I wrote them down, and reading them back, it sounds like a fantasy story. Yet it was as real as walking down the street and seeing a tree. I experienced Ramana Maharshi, even an Egyptian God named Horus who I didn't even know existed. He appeared with a dog's head, and I had to ask my wife, who knows more about Egyptian mythology than I do, who he was. Seems he is the guardian of the underworld. It was divine presence showing me the gates of death, and that opened deeper dimensions of both death and life.

Here is Lahana Grey, from Canada:

I had never felt as fully free as I dreamed I could be. I knew love, I knew meditation, I knew God—but things were still arising to cause discomfort, and I didn't know how to deal with it. During the program, we were in meditation, at the start of a ceremony. I just prayed and prayed. I said, "Please, Amma Bhagavan, please show me what devotion really feels like." Before I knew it, I was up and starting to dance. I was so moved and pulled and pulled. These flowers were put in my hand, and I shook, and I knew I was holding the living God in my own hands. I was so overwhelmed. By the time I poured the flowers into the bowl, I felt the living force so powerfully, it hit me, and I was shaking, and I wanted to howl and scream. I held it in, but I was trapped—I didn't know where to go because I was kind of stuck between all the people. But someone saw me and created a space so that I could move with this living force, and I just fell upon the ground, and I was cracked. I was just cracked like a coconut. I split open. Everything fell out, and I learned how to pray, and I sought and prayed to Amma Bhagavan to free me. It was wonderful.

Finally, here is Nahuel Schajris, the Grammy Award-winning musician from Argentina:

God is the air that I breathe, every time I breathe. God is when I brush my teeth. God is when I play music. God is when I see a beautiful sunset. God is when I argue with someone. God is when we meet. God is when I'm feeling pain. This amazing formless, limitless God! There are endless forms of God. You choose whatever you want. You can choose whatever form, whatever experience, whatever way, to be connected with that amazing creative power. And that's God. God is in everything. I relate with Amma and Bhagavan as forms of God, because I really like them. But you can relate to God as a flame of fire, as a voice within you, as a wind, as Buddha, as Jesus, as Allah, whatever you want. God is not an absolute thing. It's a subjective experience. We have to understand that. God is not an absolute thing. It's not a man or a woman. It's everything. It's everything. So what is God to you? That's the question. We are creators, too. We are creating our lives all the time. We are creating everything. That's why we are in the image of God, made in the image of God, because we are also creators.

It is in the same way, as a creator, that you can let the story of the Oneness Blessing settle now in your heart. In these pages, you have heard some wild and wonderful stories from people all over the world, whose lives have changed in all kinds of ways. If these were only stories of an occasional miraculous healing here or there or of a few people having mystical visions, this phenomenon would be easier to pigeonhole. It is the sheer magnitude and variety of these stories, and the very short time in which they have all taken place, that makes the Oneness Blessing an enigma. This mysterious Blessing is not an absolute thing; it can also be everything. So what will the Oneness Blessing become for you?

That is the question.

EPILOGUE

I come from a family of writers. My father was a journalist for *The Times* of London when I was born, and he went on to write twenty-two books. My mother was, at one time, acquisitions editor for Faber and Faber, one of England's most reputable publishers. My childhood unfolded to the soundtrack of the tap-tapping of typewriter keys. I spent the early part of my adult life in a vain attempt to resist this genetic inheritance, but by age thirty-five, those efforts were exhausted—I came to accept that I was just another chip off the family block of wordsmiths, and wrote my first book.

I was raised with an unspoken code that writers, particularly writers of nonfiction works like this one, need a certain degree of objectivity to be able to do their job well. Just like for a psychotherapist, a doctor, or a lawyer, it's not professional to fall in love with your subject. My father cultivated a disposition of amused, but detached, interest toward the world. He would stand on the sidelines of the game—other peoples' game. Skepticism was not a malaise in his universe; it was an absolute and unquestioned necessity. Maintaining this kind of objectivity in writing this book about Amma, Bhagavan, and the Oneness Blessing has been a great test—one which I have probably failed.

The thing is, you see, I have two sons: one is eleven, and one is fourteen. I love them to bits. I care deeply about the quality of the air they and their children will breathe. I care about the kind of economic system they will inherit. I care about the planet we leave them and their generation. I care deeply and passionately about giving them the best chance we can. Most people today recognize that we face various crises of unprecedented proportions: global warming, depletion of oil, wars of fundamentalism. The only thing they all have in common is that we do not have ready solutions for any of them. The future looks a little wobbly. Remember Einstein: you cannot solve any problem in the same state of consciouness in which it was created. The world is crying out for a change of heart, a quantum leap from one state of consciousness to another. Our future likely depends on it.

This is a big deal. If it was the basement of your house that had dry rot, it might be different. You could always try to get it repaired. If it was beyond repair, you could move, and the insurance might even kick in. If it was the neighborhood in which you lived, you could move to another part of the city. You could always move to another city altogether, another state, even another country. But when it's the planet on which we live that is in crisis, it becomes more serious. Most of us have no reliable awareness of anything else. This is it. This is home. This is all that we have stored in our memory banks.

When you read about a temple in southern India costing US$17 million to house eight thousand "cosmic beings" who are going to save the world, it's easy to be skeptical. Inevitable, actually. When you hear about another Indian organization and another Indian teacher, it's easy to be overcome by a flashback to the '60s, or the '70s, or even the '80s, and to be dismissive. When you hear about young Westerners, many of them new to spirituality, popping over to India for a three-week visit and coming back claiming to be fully enlightened, it's easy to roll one's eyes to the ceiling and dismiss it as another symptom of a culture craving instant gratification. There are probably hundreds of good reasons, when you hear about this phenomenon, to be dismissive.

It is that once you have tasted the strawberry, rather than just reading about tasting it, it becomes more difficult to keep up that hard-earned skepticism. If you are hearing about the Oneness Blessing for the first time here, I have no ambitions that this book should convince you on the first read. My hope is that what is presented in these pages will simply be enough for you to offer this phenomenon the benefit of the doubt. My hope is that these pages may have kindled enough interest in you to want to find out for yourself from direct experience.

My guess is that, just like me, you probably care about this world. Just like me, you may have children. Just like me, you may also have a deep, but buried, intuition for what could be possible for human life, for your life, for our lives. Just like me, you may have a forgotten cellular memory of the perfume of true freedom from the mind, of a sense of causeless love and well-being that wants to give itself as a blessing through you. It may be that what has been written in these pages could inspire you to find out a little more about how this could be possible. Then, just like me, it might be that something in you is touched, something more eloquent and trustworthy than our armor of cynicism. Finally, you will come to know the truth about this phenomenon, not from the logic of the mind, but from the wisdom of the heart.

May all beings be well.

May all beings be happy.

May all beings be free from suffering.

May all beings be liberated through the unwavering knowledge of who they truly are.

Arjuna Ardagh
Nevada City, California
1 January 2007

ACKNOWLEDGMENTS

The entire process of researching and writing this book happened in a relatively short period of time, under what sometimes seemed to be insurmountable odds. Although I was invited to write a book in December 2005, I wasn't free to begin the first interviews until April 2006. During the following months, I talked to several hundred Blessing givers and recipients all over the world, by phone and in person.

None of this would have been possible without the extraordinarily generous help of my good friends, Glenn Hovemann and Muffy Weaver. They own a successful children's book publishing company of their own and have plenty to do. But when they heard about this project, they put body and soul into helping me track down the right people to talk to, scheduling appointments, and dealing with the fallout when the connection to a cell phone in the Ukraine didn't work or a Hollywood celebrity didn't pick up his phone for the fourth time in a row. I'm immensely grateful to Muffy and Glenn and bow to their self-effacing magnitude of heart.

Every one of the hundreds of interviews needed to be transcribed so that we could choose the very best and include them in the book. This mammoth work was done by Sandra Clark of Rivercrest Business Services in Texas. On some occasions, she turned around hours of recorded material in less than a day. If you find yourself one day needing to write a book based on hundreds of hours of telephone interviews, Sandra is your gal.

And, of course, I am very grateful to the people all over the world who gave so generously of their time in sharing with me their experience of the Oneness Blessing.

On the home front, I am, as always, grateful beyond words to my family. My wife, Chameli, who is an accomplished writer and teacher in her own right, took on the greater part of the household duties during these months to free me up to meet the deadline. And my sons, Abhi and Shuba, were superbly understanding when, yet again, Dad had to spend the weekend shackled to his laptop in the office. Our manager, Garrett Stanley, has become a part of the family now. He held down the fort. He answered my e-mail. He took care of all the practical sides of life, leaving me undisturbed.

Tami Simon has become not just my publisher but a truly beloved friend and dharma sister. She was, from the beginning, magnificently open to this phenomenon, although she knew nothing about it. She and her company are every writer's dream. This goes not only for Tami, but for all the people without exception who work with her—including my editor, Kelly Notaras; Tara Lupo, assistant to the publisher; Chantal Pierrat, director of sales and marketing; Haven Iverson, production editor; Karen Polaski, art director; Lisa Kerans, designer; Tara Joffe, copyeditor; and Marjorie Woodall and Marj Hahne, proofreaders.

But I reserve the peaks of my gratitude for the folks in India, who have become like family: Acharya Samadarshini, Acharya Anandagiri, Sneha, Krishnaraj, Aravind, Radhakrishna, Pragyanand, and all the dasas who pulled out all the stops to get me everything I needed, whenever I needed it.

Words fall short in the gratitude I feel to the mystery that is Sri Amma Bhagavan. On the surface it seems like I met an Indian couple in their fifties who had at one time owned a school. Through the process of writing this book, I've come to discover there's much more to it than that, something more in the realm of magic. Whenever I met with Bhagavan in interviews or personal conversations, it never really felt like I was meeting a person. It felt more like I was talking to the sky or to the ocean, or perhaps to my own heart, unfettered by the mind.

RESOURCES

As this manuscript goes to press in March 2007, it is a strange feeling to know that by the time you read it, it will already be out of date. This phenomenon is expanding and changing so fast that there would be no way to create a book that was still current by the time it hit the bookshelves.

For this reason, this book has its very own website: www.awakening intooneness.org. On the site you will be able to find out about more recent news, including brain research, the Hundred Village Project, and the effect of the Oneness Blessing on businesses, schools, and government. In addition, the website will help you to locate a Blessing giver in your area and inform you about events connected with this book.

To find out more about the Oneness University in India, please visit their website, www.onenessuniversity.org.

For information about the Oneness Blessing in North America and Canada, please visit www.onenessmovement.org.

Both of the above sites contain links to Oneness websites in other languages for other parts of the world.

For more information about the work of Alexis Shaffer in Mexico, her website is www.livinginoneness.com.

For more information about Johan Mansson, who has been using the Oneness Blessing to help young drug addicts (pages 73 and 108), you can e-mail him at beroendehealing@spray.se.

For more information about Dr. Sunil Joshi, the Ayurvedic doctor (page 68), please visit www.vinayakayurveda.com.

For more information about Bruhn and Cecile Henriksen (page 75), please visit www.onenesscenter.org.

ABOUT
THE AUTHOR

Arjuna Ardagh is the founder of the Living Essence Foundation in Nevada City, California, a nonprofit church dedicated to the awakening of consciousness within the context of ordinary life. He is the author of *The Translucent Revolution, Relaxing into Clear Seeing, How About Now?*, and *The Last Laugh* (a novel). He is the host of the *Awakening into Oneness* DVD series, and the creator of *Let Yourself Go* (a six-CD audio set), the *Living Essence Audio Series, Living Essence Live,* and many other audio and video products.

Ardagh was educated in England, at Kings School, Canterbury, and later at Cambridge University, where he earned a master's degree in literature. Since the age of fourteen, he has had a passionate interest in spiritual awakening, and he began to practice meditation and yoga at that time. In his late teens, he trained as a meditation teacher. After graduating from Cambridge, Ardagh devoted himself completely to the call he felt inside, and he studied and lived with a number of great spiritual teachers, both in Asia and in the United States. In 1987 he founded the Alchemy Institute in Seattle, Washington, and trained several hundred people in a transpersonal approach to hypnotherapy.

In 1991 he returned to India for a period of prolonged meditation and met H. W. L. Poonjaji, a direct devotee of the great sage Ramana Maharshi, with whom he went through a radical awakening. After returning to the United States, Ardagh began to share this awakened view with other people at Poonjaji's request, facilitating a dramatic shift in awareness with thousands of people throughout the United States and Europe. In 1995 Ardagh developed the Living Essence Training, which prepares people to be facilitators of this shift in consciousness and to cultivate translucence.

Ardagh was invited to the Oneness University in the winter of 2005, which initiated the conception of this book. He now integrates the Oneness Blessing (deeksha) into all the other work he does. He speaks at many international conferences, and has appeared on TV, on the radio, and in print media in twelve countries. He also teaches the Deeper Love seminars with his Norwegian wife, Chameli Gad Ardagh. They live in Nevada City with his two sons. You may contact him at:

Arjuna@awakeningintooneness.org
www.awakeningintooneness.org
www.livingessence.com
www.translucents.org

ABOUT
SOUNDS TRUE

Sounds True was founded in 1985 with a clear vision: to disseminate spiritual wisdom. Located in Boulder, Colorado, Sounds True publishes teaching programs that are designed to educate, uplift, and inspire. With more than 550 titles available, we work with many of the leading teachers, thinkers, healers, and visionary artists of our time.

For a free catalog of wisdom teachings for the inner life, please contact Sounds True via the World Wide Web at www.soundstrue.com, call us toll-free at 800-333-9185, or write

The Sounds True Catalog
PO Box 8010
Boulder CO 80306